John Keble, Edward Bouverie Pusey

Sermons on the Litany, the Church One, Catholic, Apostolic, Holy and the Communion of Saints

John Keble, Edward Bouverie Pusey

Sermons on the Litany, the Church One, Catholic, Apostolic, Holy and the Communion of Saints

ISBN/EAN: 9783744742238

Printed in Europe, USA, Canada, Australia, Japan

Cover: Foto ©Lupo / pixelio.de

More available books at **www.hansebooks.com**

SERMONS ON THE LITANY

THE CHURCH ONE,

CATHOLIC, APOSTOLIC AND HOLY

AND

THE COMMUNION OF SAINTS

REPRINTED FROM 'SERMONS FOR THE CHRISTIAN YEAR

BY THE LATE

REV. JOHN KEBLE
AUTHOR OF 'THE CHRISTIAN YEAR'

WITH INTRODUCTORY NOTICE BY THE LATE
REV. E. B. PUSEY, D.D.

LONDON
WALTER SMITH (LATE MOZLEY)
34 KING STREET, COVENT GARDEN
1885

ADVERTISEMENT.

THIS course of Sermons on the Litany is a good example of Mr. Keble's way of explaining and drawing instruction from the Church Services. He first catechised the children upon them, and then summed up the lessons given, in his Sermon. They exhibit in a very striking manner, the "plainness of speech" which it was his wont to use, in pastoral warnings and instructions, on subjects where plainness is always a difficulty, and must have cost no small effort. Every word of John Keble, if weighed, evinces, in its simplicity, the depth of his reality. But to see in mind the Sexagenarian (as he then was) finding his way with his lantern at 5.30 A.M. on Wednesdays and Fridays, sometimes in snow, on winter mornings, to say the Litany[1] for the

---

[1] It was so said from May or June 1850, until the autumn of 1853. He used to remain for half-an-hour or an hour in the Church afterwards. He himself alludes to it below in the first Introductory Address on the Litany, p. 7.

Church in "her present distress," will bring home what the Litany was to him. Sometimes there was only one other worshipper. But a Third was there, Who said, "Where *two* or three are gathered together in My Name, there am I in the midst of them."

E. B. P.

CHRIST CHURCH,
Epiphany, 1879.

CONTENTS.

SERMON I.

On the Litany. I.—Introductory, and on the Invocation of the Holy Trinity.

Joel ii. 17.   PAGE

Let the priests, the ministers of the Lord, weep between the porch and the Altar, and let them say, Spare Thy people, O Lord   1

SERMON II.

On the Litany. II.—On the special Invocation of our Lord in the ' Remember not,' etc.

Joel ii. 17.

Let the priests, the ministers of the Lord, weep between the porch and the Altar, and let them say, Spare Thy people, O Lord, and give not Thine heritage to reproach, that the heathen should rule over them   .   13

SERMON III.

On the Litany. III.—The Deprecation.

2 *Chron.* vi. 28-30.   PAGE

Whatsoever sore or whatsoever sickness there be: what prayer or what supplication soever shall be made of any man, or of all Thy people Israel, when every one shall know his own sore and his own grief, and shall spread forth his hands in this house; then hear Thou from heaven, Thy dwelling place, and forgive . .   24

SERMON IV.

On the Litany. IV.

2 *Thess.* iii. 3.

The Lord is faithful, Who shall stablish you, and keep you from evil   35

SERMON V.

On the Litany. V.

Heb. ii. 14, 15.

Forasmuch then as the children are partakers of flesh and blood, He also Himself likewise took part of the same; that through death He might destroy him that had the power of death, that is, the devil; and deliver them who through fear of death were all their lifetime subject to bondage   47

Contents.

SERMON VI.

On the Litany. VI.—The Intercessions.

1 *Tim.* ii. 1, 2.   PAGE

I exhort therefore, that, first of all, supplications, prayers, intercessions, and giving of thanks, be made for all men ; for kings, and for all that are in authority ; that we may lead a quiet and peaceable life in all godliness and honesty   60

SERMON VII.

On the Litany. VII.—The Private Intercessions.

Heb. xiii. 18.

Pray for us : for we trust we have a good conscience, in all things willing to live honestly   71

SERMON VIII.

On the Litany. VIII.—The Suffrages.

Heb. vii. 25.

He is able to save them to the uttermost that come unto God by Him, seeing He ever liveth to make intercession for them   83

SERMON IX.

On the Litany. IX.—Conclusion.

Psalm xxxiii. 22.

Let Thy merciful kindness, O Lord, be upon us, like as we do put our trust in Thee   96

SERMON X.

The Church One.

1 *S. John* v. 8.

There are three that bear witness in earth, the Spirit, and the water, and the Blood; and these three agree in one   110

SERMON XI.

The Church Catholic.

1 *Tim.* ii. 4.

Who will have all men to be saved, and to come to the knowledge of the Truth 124

SERMON XII.

The Church Apostolic.

Deut. v. 31.

Stand thou here by Me, and I will speak unto thee all the commandments 137

SERMON XIII.

The Church Holy.

Deut. vii. 6.

Thou art an holy people unto the Lord thy God.   149

SERMON XIV.

The Communion of Saints. S. Philip and S. James' Day.

S. James i. 18.

Of His own will begat He us with the word of truth, that we should be a kind of first-fruits of His creatures   160

SERMON I.

ON THE LITANY. I.

INTRODUCTORY, AND ON THE INVOCATION OF THE
HOLY TRINITY.

JOEL ii. 17.

Let the priests, the ministers of the Lord, weep between the porch and the Altar, and let them say, Spare Thy people, O Lord.

I HAVE thought it might be good for us, my brethren, during this Epiphany season, to go over the Prayer-book, by catechizing the children in it as we did with the Baptism service last year. And I have chosen the Litany; a portion of the service which I am sure must be very dear to us all, if we really are used to attend to the solemn service of God : and concerning which it was said by one of the best and wisest of our forefathers, that it is 'a work, the absolute perfection whereof upbraideth with error or something worse those whom in all parts it doth not satisfy.'

How the Litany differs from the ordinary sort of prayers, is easy enough for us to understand. It is a *general* supplication : i.e. a form of prayer in which all the people join, not by saying it all after the minister, as we do the Lord's prayer, and certain confessions of sin : nor yet by only saying Amen at the end of each short wish; as we do in most of the collects: but by a short verse, repeated at certain intervals, and breaking into a number of short portions what would otherwise be a very long prayer to be said all at once. The rule and beginning of such a service may be found in the Old Testament, especially in that very aweful and serious chapter of the prophet Joel, from which the text is taken. The prophet is speaking of a host of terrible enemies, who might soon be looked for to overspread and ruin the land: which prophecy seems to have been fulfilled partly in a frightful swarm of locusts, who should come upon the sinful land, partly in an invasion from some unpitying enemy; such as the Assyrian at that time, the Roman long after, and it may be, in the Last Day, some other power worse and more wicked than both these. At such a time the Spirit of God directed the old Church of the Jews to seek mercy and help of God by special and very solemn services in which the whole people should join. First, the people were to repent, each one inwardly in his heart, each family in its quiet home. 'Therefore also now, saith the Lord, turn ye even to Me with all your heart, and with fasting, and with weeping, and with mourning: and rend your heart and not your garments, and turn unto the Lord your God.' That was to be each man's preparation of heart in those evil times: unfeigned sorrow for his sin, self-denial, and punishing the flesh, and true conversion to God, as to an offended but loving Father. But not only was each one so to be prepared inwardly in his heart, and in his devotions privately and at home, but publickly also the whole Church was to join in solemn acknowledgment of sin, and in beseeching God to turn away His judgements from the land. 'Blow the trumpet,' he says, 'in Zion, sanctify a fast, call a solemn assembly; gather the people, sanctify the congregation, assemble the elders, gather the children and those that suck the breasts: let the bridegroom go forth of his chamber, and the bride out of her closet.' You see, even those who might be best excused from attending public services, little children, and those who waited on them, and also new married people, were expected to attend the particular service of which the prophet was speaking. And what was that service? It was a Litany. The priests, the Lord's ministers, were to take their places in the temple, between the porch and the Altar, i. e. in some such place as the entrance of our chancel, where, as you know, we kneel to say the Litany. There the priests were to kneel and weep, i. e. they were both outwardly in voice and behaviour, and inwardly in heart and soul, to show how grieved they were, and how deeply they felt God's anger and their own sinfulness. And what was their prayer to be? God Himself put a word in their mouth, in that He taught them to say, 'Spare Thy people, O Lord, and give not Thine heritage to reproach, that the heathen should rule over them: wherefore should they say among the people, Where is their God?' This was the service prescribed by the Almighty to His ancient people in time of trouble: and see what encouragement He gave them to perform it religiously. 'Then' (so He expressly promises), 'Then will the Lord be jealous for His land, and pity His people.' He will, as in former times, interfere to prevent their being ill-used (for that is what it means when He says He will be jealous for them): and for all their sins, He will pity them in their sad distresses. So great was the benefit to be hoped for of old from such a service as our Litany, provided only it were earnestly attended by the people in general with a true penitent heart.

And is the Lord's hand waxed short? May we not hope for the same blessing now? We Christians as well as those Jews—the members of Christ, as well as the children of Israel? Surely we may: the Christian Litany will not be less favoured than the Jewish. I say, the Christian Litany: for this is one of those

On the Litany. I.

Services which the Church of Christ from very early times has taken to be its own, out of the Old Testament. For thus it was, brethren. More than thirteen hundred years ago, when the old Roman Empire was in a most miserable condition, the wild savages attacking it on every side, and God's dreadful judgements coming upon it in sword, in famine, and in pestilence: it came into the mind of a holy Bishop to gather the people of his flock together, and make a solemn procession with prayers after the manner of our Litany, and according to the recommendation of the prophet Joel. The people readily came into it, and the custom spread from one place to another: and though at first it belonged especially to the three days which come next before Ascension Day (which we therefore call Rogation days, or days of special prayer), it was by no means confined to those days, but was generally practised in times of trouble, to the great comfort of God's people, and often with a manifest blessing from Him. This then being a very ancient and godly custom of the Church, when our English Prayer-book was put in order about three hundred years ago, order was taken that it should be kept up among us, by the saying of the Litany in the Church three times a week, i.e. on Sundays, Wednesdays, and Fridays, and at such other times as the Bishop shall direct. And this, for the obtaining pardon of our manifold sins, and turning away God's heavy judgements, too likely to fall upon us. And Wednesday and Friday were fixed upon, I suppose, because from the beginning they have been the penitential days of the Church: Wednesday, as being that day of the week in which Judas made his bargain to betray our Saviour; Friday, as being the day of our Saviour's death. And Sunday was added afterwards, as we may suppose, because it is the day when most people come to Church: and seeing that the Church is altogether in a fallen state, compared with its first days, it seems well that even her Sundays, her glad and good times, should be marked with this exercise of penitence: even as she begins her daily services with the most humble confession of sins. But indeed since the world at all times is full enough of sin and misery; God dishonoured everywhere, and man afflicted; there is always reason enough for saying of Litanies. However, it has seemed to me especially seasonable just now. For we seem to be, in some sort, in the midst or on the edge of many troubles, both spiritual and temporal. It is a season, not so much of sharp sickness, and such as is known to be dangerous, but of lowness, and weakness, and helplessness: as if many persons, though not quite ill, were on the verge of being so. And in fact, on counting our burials of the past year, I find more of us have passed out of this world than in any one year, the accounts of which I have had occasion to examine. We may therefore, in a manner, apply to ourselves S. Paul's saying to his Corinthian children: '[a] Many are weak and sickly among us, and many sleep.' Death, my brethren, is and has been knocking at our doors: very gently and mercifully it is true, yet very distinctly. And then we hear of a good deal of distress among many of our brethren: and I doubt not we hear truly. The poverty and misery may not, by God's mercy, be so great here as in many other places. But who can doubt that there is in the land poverty and misery enough to make it the duty of all charitable people to pray for their brethren who are so tried? Even for our temporal and worldly condition, therefore, there seems great reason why we should be quite in earnest in saying our Litanies at this time. But for the spiritual condition of our English Church, believe me, my brethren, when I tell you that it is indeed very distressing. We are hard beset on both sides: and why? Because people have not the faith which they ought to have in the blessed Sacraments of Christ, whereby He both received us at first, and hath fed us all our lives long unto this day. Some persons do not like to believe that holy Baptism saves us at all, although the Prayer-book teaches it so plainly: and these unhappily have so great power at present, that

[a] 1 Cor. xi. 30.

there is great danger of their altering the words of the Prayer-book, as they have already perverted its doctrine. These, it is plain, have no faith in the Sacraments of Christ. Others are so disgusted at seeing such liberties taken with such very holy things that they begin to think the Body which allows them can be no part of the true Church of Christ, and so they wander away to the Roman Catholics; not considering, that in so doing they are giving up all faith in the holy Sacraments which have been their soul's health hitherto. These two sorts, unlike as they appear to each other, agree in this, that neither of them has faith in what Christ has done for them: and between these two, as I said, our mother the Church is even now hard beset; and if her hope and strength were of this world only, I cannot say how it would be with her. But, my brethren, 'ᵇ God is our Hope and Strength.' Only we must call upon God, for He loves to be called upon: His Title is 'ᶜ Thou that hearest the prayer.' This is why we have endeavoured of late to have more Litanies in the parish: to give those who fear God and believe His Sacraments and love His Church a chance of calling upon Him in the early morning, while they are on their way to their day's work. We have said to ourselves, 'What if God in answer even to such weak prayers should begin to be gracious to

ᵇ Ps. xlvii. 1. ᶜ Ps. lxv. 2.

His land, and to pity His people? and to restore to us the blessings which our own sins, and Evil powers, seem to be depriving us of?' And so, for several months past, twice a week, in the early morning, sometimes in light, and sometimes in darkness, the sound has gone up here, 'Spare us, good Lord; spare Thy people, whom Thou hast redeemed with Thy most precious Blood: and be not angry with us.' The words have gone up, and even if it were, as far as man could see, from a very few, yet may we hope that it has not been all in vain. We may hope that some have thought of that early Litany, and may have been the better for it, though other duties prevented their coming near it. They may have profited in ways that we know not of. The very sound of the bells may have done them good, as they were preparing for their day's work, or resting on their bed of infirmity. And our Lord's promise does not require a large congregation. It is given to two or three, gathered together in His Name. The Angels, we trust, keep watch in this house: and '[d] there is joy in the presence of the Angels of God over one sinner that repenteth.' Therefore, if it please God, we hope to go on with that early Litany, at least during the present distress of the Church: and *that*, in all probability, will last more years than we shall in this world. And may God in-

[d] S. Luke xv. 10.

crease the number of those who delight in such holy and regular services, whether they can attend them or no.

There is one reason why our Litany is particularly fit to begin the services of the day : which is, the way in which it begins: we begin it with commending ourselves to the most Holy Trinity in whose Name we were sealed in Baptism. As we began our whole Christian life, so it is well to begin each separate day, under the shadow and protection of that saving Name : it comes into our Litany, as the Name Jehovah into the Litany of the Jews: 'Spare Thy people, good Lord, spare them.' But we first acknowledge and seal the Church's full doctrine, how that They are three real Persons, distinguished as in the Creed of S. Athanasius: The First, God the Father of heaven; The Second, God the Son, Redeemer of the world; The Third, God the Holy Ghost, proceeding from the Father and the Son: yet one only God, All-Holy, Blessed, and Glorious : and how that before each of the Three Persons, as also before the Holy, Blessed and Glorious Trinity, which is the Three taken together, we, one and all, are miserable sinners, and can only approach Him as such, humbly pleading for His mercy.

Such is the great Invocation, as you may call it, with which our Litany begins: even as it ends with a blessing in the Name of the same Divine Persons: 'The grace of our Lord Jesus Christ, the love of God, and the fellowship of the Holy Ghost.' For such as is the kingdom of God itself, such are all the services which we are permitted to do for Him in His kingdom: they all begin and end in the same Holy Name; the Name of the most Blessed and Glorious Trinity. Let us by His grace bear the remembrance of that Name always with us about the world. The Name itself we cannot but carry with us: it was stamped on us at our Baptism, never to be worn out: we may neglect, disgrace, insult it, but never can we be as the heathen who never had part in it. Miserable sinners indeed we are, and shall be to our lives' end: our birth from Adam makes that certain, to say nothing of our own backslidings: but that need not keep us from Him: only may we always take care to mean what we say when we call ourselves by that title: for many, I fear, are in the way of kneeling before God and saying the Litany regularly, who in the bottom of their hearts neither count themselves miserable nor sinners, but think they are as good as other people, and have a right to all the enjoyment they can get in this world. May God deliver us from so trifling with His blessed yet awful invitation, since He invites us thrice a week to come to Him, miserable sinners as we are; to come to the Holy, Blessed and Glorious Three Persons and

One God, and to call upon Him for mercy; let us at least come with serious, thoughtful hearts. To join in saying the Litany is a great gift, a great privilege, a noble chance of obtaining a blessing for ourselves and for the whole Church. To say it coldly, inattentively, disrespectfully, wilfully to slight it in any way, is behaving as if God were not God, as if we were not sinners. And how then can we be forgiven or blessed?

SERMON II.

ON THE LITANY. II.

ON THE SPECIAL INVOCATION OF OUR LORD IN THE
'REMEMBER NOT,' ETC.

JOEL ii. 17.

Let the priests, the ministers of the Lord, weep between the porch and the Altar, and let them say, Spare Thy people, O Lord, and give not Thine heritage to reproach, that the heathen should rule over them.

HAVING, in the first Invocation, or beginning of the Litany, called upon the most Holy Trinity, Three Persons, and One God, and humbled ourselves in that aweful Presence as miserable sinners, we go on to pray against sundry evils, and to ask sundry blessings of God. But first of all we turn as it were to our blessed Redeemer Jesus Christ, and put our cause into His hands: we turn to Him as to God Incarnate, God made manifest in the flesh, because we know that He can be touched with a feeling of our infirmities. Apart from Him we should not have boldness to enter into that glorious Presence. It would be far stranger than for the meanest beggar to press forward with a petition to the proudest and greatest monarch. But as it is, we may and must come, for we are invited, nay commanded to come. 'Come unto Me,' says the Divine Intercessor, 'all ye that labour and are heavy laden, and I will give you rest.' 'Him that cometh to Me, I will in no wise cast out.' Therefore we are bold to come to Christ, to Him our only appointed Mediator, and by Him, miserable sinners as we are, to be spared, cleansed and forgiven.

And mark how we plead with Him. The prophet instructs the ancient people, when they were saying their Litany, to cry out unto Christ and say, 'Spare Thy people, O Lord, spare them, and let not Thine heritage be brought to confusion.' That was his plea, the plea of the good Israelite: the plea which Moses, a thousand years before, had alleged, when interceding with God to pardon them for making the golden calf. 'ᵃ O Lord God,' saith Moses, 'destroy not Thy people, nor Thine inheritance, which Thou hast redeemed through Thy greatness, which Thou hast brought forth out of Egypt with a mighty hand: Remember Thy servants, Abraham, Isaac, and Jacob: look not unto the stubbornness of this people, nor to their iniquity, nor to their sin. . . Yet they are Thy people and Thine inheritance, which Thou broughtest out by Thy mighty power

ᵃ Deut. ix. 26-29.

and by Thy stretched out Arm.' You see, the prophets allege to God, not any good thing which His people had ever done, but His mercy showed unto them. They put Him in mind how He brought them out of Egypt: how He had chosen them to be His own people. So we in our Litany, approaching our Lord and Judge. We have no good thing of our own to plead, nothing but sins and offences, of our own and our forefathers, which we beseech Him not to remember. But what we *do* plead is, His past and present mercy shown to us. 'Spare us, good Lord, spare Thy people, whom Thou hast redeemed with Thy most precious Blood.' 'Spare us, not because we are good, but because we are Thy people. We are Christians, Thine own people, Thine own heritage. This was Thy special, Thy distinguishing mercy to us, to choose us freely, before the world began, to be Christians, members of Christ. Forsake not then, we beseech Thee, the work of Thine own hands. As Thou hast begun to do us good, so go on with us even to the end.'

Again, we see how the prophets make mention of what God's enemies would say, if the Israelites, His people, were quite forsaken. 'Wherefore should they say among the people, Where is their God?' And Moses' word is, 'Spare them, lest the Egyptians say, The Lord was not able to bring them into the land which He promised them.' So we Christians pray in the Psalms, '[b] Lighten mine eyes that I sleep not in death, lest mine enemy say, I have prevailed against him, for if I be cast down, they that trouble me will rejoice at it.' In all these prayers, you see, we plead with God by His own glory and honour, not by any good or merit of ours.

But more especially do we Christians plead with Him by what He did and suffered for us upon the Cross. 'Spare Thy people, whom Thou hast redeemed with Thy most precious Blood.' As if we should say, 'Thou didst sacrifice Thyself entirely for us, Body and Soul. Thou pouredst out Thy Blood without stint or measure from Thy five healing Wounds. Thou didst grudge for our salvation no pain or grief, no agony or anguish of heart: Thou didst mysteriously become poor, emptying Thyself that we might be filled with Thee. And now, we beseech Thee, let it not be all in vain, miserably as we have behaved, shamefully as we have trifled with Thy loving salvation, do Thou yet find some way of making it effectual to us.' This is the Church's prayer to our Saviour when she is on her knees before Him in humble confession. And then she goes on, one by one, to mention those evils by name against which she most earnestly desires to pray; such as sin, the crafts and assaults of the devil, God's

[b] Ps. xiii. 3.

On the Litany. II.

wrath, everlasting damnation, and the rest: teaching her children to make answer from time to time, 'Good Lord, deliver us.'

But before we go on to consider this, there are a few more observations to be made on this first invocation to our Lord. It begins, you know, with the word Remember: 'Remember not, Lord, our offences, nor the offences of our forefathers.' This is not said as if God could ever forget: for we know that past, present, and future are all alike to Him. But it is taken from a verse in the Psalms: 'c Remember not our old sins, but have mercy upon us, and that soon, for we are come to great misery.' So also the holy Nehemiah, 'd Remember me, O my God, for good:' three times in one chapter. And in another Psalm, 'e Remember me, O Lord, according to the favour that Thou bearest unto Thy people.' And Moses, 'Remember Abraham, Isaac, and Israel Thy servants.' And 'Lord, remember David and all his trouble.' And in the history: 'God remembered Rachel:' 'God remembered Abraham:' 'God remembered Noah:' and so in many other places. It is not, as I said, that the all-knowing God can ever possibly forget or be ignorant: but it is His gracious will that we should address Him in such words. Even as it is His will, that in the sacrifice of the Holy Communion

c Ps. lxxix. 8.   d Neh. xiii. 14, 22, 31.
e Ps. cvi. 4.

we should offer to Him His own appointed Memorial of the One atoning Sacrifice, offered once for all on the Cross, and continually presented to Him by our great High Priest in heaven. The Holy Communion, as the Prayer-book teaches out of our Lord's own Mouth, is a perpetual memory of our Lord's precious Death: not only as putting us in mind of it, but also as putting God in mind of it: that is to say, pleading it before Him. By the Holy Communion, we say continually, not in words but in deeds, 'Remember not, Lord, our sins, nor the sins of our forefathers, but remember Thy well-beloved Son's offering of His Sacred Body and Blood, which in spirit and mystery we now present before Thee, as He commanded: and for His sake be merciful unto us.' In short our action in celebrating that Sacrament has the same kind of meaning, but greatly more virtue, than our words when we end prayers and collects by saying, 'through the merits and mediation of Jesus Christ our Lord.' And thus you may understand how it pleases Almighty God to be asked to remember us for good, and not to remember our sins, although in very deed He never can forget anything.

Next I may observe that the Church instructs us here to mention not our own sins only, but the sins of those also who have gone before us. 'Remember not, Lord, our offences, nor the offences of our forefathers.' Who are our forefathers, whose offences we here beseech God not to remember? In the first place, most likely, our first parents after the flesh, Adam and Eve; who by their great offence brought sin and death into the world. We all know that many, i.e. all of us, were made sinners by that one man and woman's disobedience: *that* sin is the root and ground of all that is unpleasant and bad to us. Divine providence remembers it against us continually: therefore we do well to pray to our Lord, thus earnestly, to deliver us from it.

In another way, no doubt, we suffer for the sins of our forefathers, inasmuch as by God's just judgement, the transgressions of the parents are many times visited on the children: as we learn in the second commandment, they who have made graven images to worship them must expect to be punished in their children. Therefore it is well for us to pray as we do in the Litany, that God would graciously spare us not only the punishment due to our own sins, but also whatever may in the course of His Providence be due to us in this world for the sins of those who have gone before us: and it is very well that we should all most earnestly seek to be delivered from the sin of Adam, the root and ground of all our misery.

From our own sins, then, and from the sins of our progenitors, and from the destruction and vengeance due to them, we beseech our Lord as it were to turn away His eyes, not to think of the sin, nor to bring the vengeance on us. And we add, 'Spare us, good Lord, spare Thy people, whom Thou hast redeemed with Thy most precious Blood: and be not angry with us for ever.' What is 'Spare us?' Deal gently with us: let us alone; let Thine hand lie lightly upon us; lay no more upon us than Thou wilt make us able to bear. We indeed deserve the worst: but we are so weak and sinful, our transgressions have brought us so very low, that we cannot but cast ourselves at Thy feet, beseeching Thee to have mercy upon us. For Thou art in a way the God of the weak and sinful: Thou invitest to Thee the weary and heavy laden: and who so wearied, so heavy laden as they?

And we trust that Thou wilt spare them, for Thou, O Lord, hast redeemed them. 'Spare Thy people, whom Thou hast redeemed with Thy most precious Blood.' Thou hast given us Thy very lifeblood out of Thine heart, to wash away our sins, and to be the drink of our disordered souls: and wilt Thou not in due time freely give us all things? Surely Thou wilt deny us nothing, Who hast given us Thyself, to be our God, and all in all to us. Least of all wilt Thou deny us pardon and forgiveness of the sins we truly repent of, and grace to watch against them hereafter. 'Spare Thy people, and be not angry with us for ever.' Observe those last words. 'Be not angry with us for ever.' It would seem as if the Church were instructing us to make up our minds to *some* anger, *some* punishment on God's part: only may it please Him not to continue it for ever. We do not ask to be free from suffering: but we do ask, please God, that our suffering may be temporal, not eternal: that it may come to an end when we are taken out of the flesh. We say, as it were, 'Do not, O Lord, as an enemy, take real vengeance of our sins: but if Thou must be angry for them (and truly they have deserved the worst of Thine anger) yet be not angry with us for ever. Strike us here, that Thou mayest spare and bless us hereafter.'

Thus we pray continually: but do we really mean what we pray? I fear not always: perhaps not even very often. For only just consider, my brethren: What is it that really takes up most of your pains, most of your attention? What sort of things are they which really interest you, which you think of day and night: 'when thou sittest in thine house, and when thou walkest by the way, when thou liest down, and when thou risest up?' Are they the things of this world or the things of the world to come: the business of the soul, or of the body? Surely if we will speak the truth, the more part of us must reply to such a question as this, that the body and its concerns, the world and its cares, do in effect take up the greater part of our minds and hearts: and while we pray for heavenly things, we are but too glad to get more and more of the things of the earth. But now, God looks upon our hearts; to our secret meaning, not to our outward prayer. He sees how it is with us : and if we do not strive to mend, He will take us, may be, at our thought rather than at our word : He will give us the good things of this life which we earnestly desire, and will deny us the good things of the next, which we do not earnestly desire. God forbid that it should be so with us! but that it may not be so, that we may not lose Eternity, by gaining some little matters in time, we had need look into our hearts, our prayers and our ways, more conscientiously than we have hitherto done. We have need to consider and lay things to heart, and not let them pass away altogether like a mere dream, as if nothing were to come of them.

'Be not angry with us for ever.' Think, dear brethren, of those words. To whom are they addressed? To our own, our only Saviour : to Him Who took on Him this poor mortal life of ours, and endured it so many years, that He might lay it down for us, dying in torments. He Who loved us so dearly; can there be reason to fear that He should not only be angry with us, but angry with us for ever? Yes, indeed: there is great reason to fear it. For He came to save us, not *in* our sins, but *from* our sins : and if we will keep them, or go back to them, we must give Him up, there is no help for it. And then that loving and merciful Countenance which looked down so gently upon us when by His minister He held us in His Arms at our Baptism, will be changed into blackness and darkness and tempest; in the day when it shall be clearly revealed. It will be the Day of His Wrath, the day of the wrath of the Lamb, *His* wrath, Whose love is our only hope: and there will be no change afterwards: such as He will look upon us then, such will He continue to look on us for ever. And the Day is near: the tokens of it, to the eye of faith, are not to be doubted. It may not come in your time, but surely it is near. O then, while He gives us leave, let us one and all make haste to the place of shelter. Let us by true repentance and confession, and loving obedience, hide ourselves under His shadow, yea even in His blessed Wounds: that in us may be fulfilled the gracious word, 'f His wrath endureth but the twinkling of an eye, and in His pleasure is life; heaviness may endure for a night, but joy cometh in the morning.'

f Ps. xxx. 5.

SERMON III.

ON THE LITANY. III.

THE DEPRECATION.

2 CHRON. vi. 28-30.

Whatsoever sore or whatsoever sickness there be: what prayer or what supplication soever shall be made of any man, or of all Thy people Israel, when every one shall know his own sore and his own grief, and shall spread forth his hands in this house; then hear Thou from heaven, Thy dwelling place, and forgive.

SEE, my brethren, what encouragement Holy Scripture here gives us, to come into God's holy house, and tell Him our wants and our griefs in such prayers as the Church's Litany. For here are the words of the wise king Solomon, put into his heart by the Holy Spirit, when he was dedicating the temple which he had builded, and asking God's blessing on the prayers which should be there offered. God's Holy Spirit put the words in Solomon's heart, therefore they are in fact the words of God teaching us how to pray to Him; and the prayers which He teaches us to ask, we are sure He will hear, if we do not by some wickedness make ourselves unfit to be heard. What is it then which He here instructs us of, as concerning our prayers to Him? It is just this, that when any trouble, public or private, secret or open, comes upon us, the way to relief is, to come and spread forth our hands in God's house: which is just what we do, when we join in the Litanies of the Church. As we read of the good king Hezekiah, that when he had received the threatening letter from Sennacherib king of Assyria, he went up into the house of the Lord, and spread it before the Lord: so our wisest way is whensoever any serious trouble or trial comes upon us, either upon our souls, our bodies, or our estates, to lay it before the Lord in humble prayer, not each one by himself alone, but in union with the prayers of all God's household the Church: and this we surely do, when we join devoutly in the Litany: whether our trouble be to ourselves alone, or whether it be such as to concern the whole Church and congregation praying with us.

If you ask, in what *part* of the Litany do we more especially 'spread the letter,' the account of our afflictions, before the Lord, each one for himself, and for all, and all for each one: I should say it was in those short prayers, commonly called Suffrages, to which we are now come: wherein after our two invocations, one to the Holy and Glorious Trinity, the other to our Lord and Saviour especially, we mention before Almighty God the evils from which we pray Him to deliver us: as if little children should all together cry out to their loving Father, and beseech Him to take away whatever it was that hurt them; only that this our Father is so perfect in wisdom and love, as to know exactly what each one wants; which among all the sore evils here reckoned up and prayed against is most in the mind of each one, and which he is most in danger of. And so is fulfilled in each Christian congregation the gracious word which the Holy Ghost taught king Solomon nearly three thousand years ago: Whatsoever sore, whatsoever sickness there is among us: when each one, small and great, knowing each one the plague of his own heart, his own sore and his own grief, cometh here and lifteth up holy hands, in true penitence for all wilful sin: him the Lord heareth in heaven His dwelling-place, and forgiveth and rendereth unto every man according to all his ways: for He only '[a] knoweth the hearts of the children of men.' And observe, my brethren, His gracious and loving condescension. He knows how much good it does us to have the prayers one of another, therefore He appoints that all should pray with all and for all; all alike are to answer and

[a] 2 Chron. vi. 30.

On the Litany. III.

say with one voice, 'Good Lord, deliver us:' and at the same time, because He knows also that it is generally neither good nor pleasant for men to intermeddle with their neighbour's secret joy and sorrow: (as it is written, '[b]the heart knoweth his own bitterness, and a stranger may not intermeddle with his joy'): He has guided the Church to set down the prayers in such words as shall come home to every man, yet not draw particular attention to any. It is a most sweet mixture of sympathy and reserve. And now let us shortly consider what the things are which we thus pray our Lord to deliver us from.

'From all evil and mischief, good Lord, deliver us.' This seems at first almost too much to ask for: evil, of one sort or another, is so necessarily bound up with our portion in this world, that it sounds like presumption for any of us to pray that we may be entirely free from evil. But we *may* pray; for He has promised to take us out of this world, into a world where no evil ever was or ever can be: into the heaven of the saints and good Angels: where is no drop, no grain, no smallest atom of evil or mischief of any kind; neither the evil of sin, nor the evil of suffering: for to both these sort of things, as you know, we attribute the name of evil. We call it evil and mischief, when a person tells a lie; and we call

[b] Prov. xiv. 10.

it also evil and mischief, when he breaks a limb, or suffers any bodily pain; to both, we give the same name of evil or mischief, yet they are widely different from each other: the one is the evil of sin, the other, of suffering: against both we pray in the Litany; from both we hope to be delivered, finally and for ever, in heaven.

But more especially we pray against sin, the chief evil; that is, against the breaking of God's law: which is therefore mentioned first among evils and mischiefs, as being incomparably the most evil and mischievous of all. For it separates from God, Who otherwise can and will cure all. I would we were all better able to enter into this true lesson of the Litany, that sin, and nothing else, is the chief-evil, because sin, and nothing else, separates from God. We all own it in words: when shall we begin to own it in deeds also; to behave as if it were altogether true? That we may say this prayer with due earnestness, let us consider how in the next words the Church helps us to pray against him who is the author of sin, and also against that which always accompanies sin, and against that which is the certain end of sin. The author of sin is the devil, therefore we say, 'From the crafts and assaults of the devil, good Lord, deliver us.' From his crafts and assaults, his secret and open attacks: whether he come upon us as a declared enemy, as he came upon S. Stephen and the other martyrs of old, and as he came upon our Lord in the last of his three temptations, openly proposing to Him to fall down and worship the Evil one: or whether on the other hand he come craftily, as he commonly does now, transforming himself into the likeness of an angel of light. O, my brethren, beware of these crafts of the devil, beware of being led into sin under the notion of good nature, and pleasing those whom you ought to please: beware of cheating or stealing under pretence of providing for your wife and children: beware in short of doing evil that good may come.

Thus the Church teaches us to pray against the author of sin: next she teaches us to pray against that which is the constant companion of wilful sin; and that is, the wrath of Christ. 'From Thy wrath, good Lord, deliver us:' i.e. from the wrath of the Lamb, from His wrath Whose love is our only hope. Well may we pray to be delivered from this, for this is putting out the last ray of our light and comfort. If Christ be angry, who shall forgive? Who shall plead our forgiveness? And yet most certain it is, that He is and ever will be angry with such as go on wilfully in their sins: and vainly do we cry out so earnestly, 'From Thy wrath, good Lord, deliver us,' so long as we permit ourselves in any secret abominations, whether of the flesh or spirit.

And of this we are fearfully reminded by the last words of this petition, 'From everlasting damnation, good Lord, deliver us.' Everlasting damnation: that is the end of sin; that is the consummation of the wrath of the Lamb; as those will miserably find who go on tempting that wrath. Everlasting damnation: think of that fearful word: not *my* word, brethren, but the word of Christ and His Church, the word of our loving mother in whom we have our heavenly birth: the word of our most loving Saviour, Who laid down His life for us. He it is Who has said plainly, 'These shall go away into everlasting punishment:' Their 'worm dieth not and their fire is not quenched.' He hath said it: you cannot doubt that it is so. It is not a frightful vision, but an aweful reality. Oh, pray against it earnestly, live against it with all your might: for this is the chief evil, the evil of evils, all other evils put together. Our Lord reminds you of it continually: continually, day by day, if you are not watching and praying, you are drawing nearer and nearer to it: What if it should be your portion at last? With what horror, with what self-reproach, will you then look back upon the many warnings you have had, the many times the terrible words have rung in your ears from the Church Litany, and that you yourselves have joined in them: 'From Thy wrath and from everlasting damnation, good Lord, deliver us.' Each time it was God Almighty speaking to you as a loving Father, and offering you His good Spirit, to get out of the way of damnation if you would: and each time you put it off. Alas! what will be your thoughts of this, when all thoughts will come too late?

But as yet, God be praised, it is not too late: and that it may never be so with us, we are to pray and to fight, by God's help, not only against sin in general but against the several sorts of sin: and first against blindness of heart: which is when the eyes of men's understanding are blinded, as S. Paul says, by the god of this world, so that they cannot discern the things which belong unto their peace: the light of the glorious Gospel of Christ cannot shine into their hearts. For most true it is that when men have gone on for a certain time unwilling to see the truth, they become by God's just judgement unable to see it: they are as if they had lost the very power of thinking on the true, eternal, Divine things: heaven itself, if it were thrown open to them, would not to their eyes be anything particular to look upon; the Cross of Christ with Him crucified upon It, would be no very moving spectacle. Especially blind are such persons to their own sins, the real state of their own souls: they think with that unhappy Church in the book of Revelations; 'I am rich and increased with goods, and have need of nothing; and know not that they are wretched and miserable and poor and blind and naked.' Therefore after this 'blindness of heart' the Litany mentions three things, 'pride, vain-glory, and hypocrisy:' which mark surprisingly how little people know of themselves: that is to say, how blind they are in their hearts. For, to be proud, is surely a very great blindness of heart : just as being humble is nothing more nor less than seeing ourselves in our true light. The wise man asked, 'Why is earth and ashes proud?' and we may ask yet more seriously, Why is he proud, who has sinned, and is in danger of everlasting death? Again, vain-glory which comes next in our petitions, is also a very great and miserable blindness of heart: for it is seeing and minding what men think of you, and not seeing or minding what judgement the great Almighty God is passing upon you. What greater blindness can you well imagine than that? And hypocrisy, that fearful vice, which our Lord so particularly hated and denounced, *that* also comes of blindness of heart. A hypocrite is one who tries to make others think better of him than he deserves: and who also behaves to Almighty God as if he could deceive Him: and when a person goes on so, he is almost sure to deceive himself likewise: a strong delusion is sent upon him, whereby he believes all manner of lies : and especially this lie, that he is good enough to be saved, when if he were not blinded in heart, he would know for an absolute certainty, that dying as he now is, he would be lost for ever. Thus hypocrisy makes blindness of heart.

These sins which have been mentioned put us wrong in regard of ourselves and our God: the next sort of sins mentioned in the Litany relate rather to our dealings with other men: 'From envy, hatred, and malice, and all uncharitableness, good Lord, deliver us.' These all come of extreme blindness of heart: for what can be blinder or more stupid than to envy another, to bear him malice or hatred, or to be uncharitable towards him? as if his prosperity could hurt us, or his misery do us good. O, if we really and truly knew beforehand but ever so little of the wretchedness of giving way to such feelings, how envy and hatred indulged make a sort of hell upon earth, even *that*, apart from the hell which is to come, would cause us to pray the prayer of the Litany, 'Good Lord, deliver us from all these,' with our very heart and soul.

There is more to be said about the sins and miseries against which we fight and pray in this portion of the Litany: more than can well be said now. For the present I would say one thing: God grant it may sink deep into the heart of every one of us: and it is this: if we *pray* against all these sins and miseries, we must surely *fight* against all: our prayers will else be little better than a mockery of Him to Whom we pray. You pray against blindness of heart: then you must open the eyes of your heart: you must not keep them wilfully shut against the light of God's Truth. You pray against pride: away then with all thoughts of praising yourself in your heart and fancy. You pray against vain-glory: how dare you listen to the flattering words of men? You pray against hypocrisy: beware of deceitful dealing; beware of all dissembling with God. You pray our loving Lord to deliver you from envy, hatred, malice, and all uncharitableness: take care to put down the first harsh thought; to keep silence, yea even from the first unkind half-word. Remember these your good prayers, both to guard yourselves beforehand from sin, and to examine yourselves afterwards, and call yourselves to account for it: that you may not have to remember them hereafter, to your shame and everlasting condemnation.

SERMON IV.

ON THE LITANY. IV.

2 THESS. iii. 3.

The Lord is faithful, Who shall stablish you, and keep you from evil.

WE have seen how the Church instructs us to pray for deliverance from all evil and mischief, more especially from all sin. Now this might seem almost too bold a prayer, seeing how "ᵃ man is born to trouble, as the sparks fly upwards," and how he is shaped in wickedness and conceived by his mother in sin. Therefore Holy Scripture is very express in making us promises, and teaching us to pray: teaching us to pray, as in the Lord's Prayer, that we may be delivered, not from some evil, but from all: and making us promises like that in the text: "the Lord is faithful, Who shall stablish you and keep you from evil." He is faithful, He may be depended on, He cannot deceive, nor fail you, He would not have taught and encouraged you to ask Him to deliver you from all

ᵃ Job v. 7.

evil, if it were not His gracious purpose so to do, on your properly asking Him. Therefore the Church, both elsewhere and here in the Litany, makes bold as a loving child to ask of her Father entire deliverance: and having mentioned in a former petition the great inward and spiritual sins, which are the roots of all that is said and done wrongly—blindness of heart, pride, vain-glory and hypocrisy, envy, hatred, and malice, and all uncharitableness—she now, in the petitions on which we have been catechising to-day, prays against their outward and visible effects, whether of sin or of punishment: and first she causes us to beseech our good Lord to deliver us 'from fornication and all other deadly sin.' On which we are to take notice, first, that there is such a thing as deadly sin; sin so exceeding black and foul and poisonous, that even one act of it, wilfully and deliberately committed, kills for the time the life of the soul, separates from God, and stops the communication of His grace: so that a person dying in such a condition would have no chance of going to heaven. This is very plain from the Scriptures: as, for example, from S. John's first Epistle, "[b] There is a sin unto death: .... all unrighteousness is sin, and there is a sin not unto death." And in several places of the New Testament certain kinds of sin are reckoned up

[b] 1 S John v. 16, 17.

in which if a man dies he is sure to be lost for ever: the works of the flesh, which they who practise shall not inherit the kingdom of God. Distinct from this worst sort of sin is that which is sometimes called venial or pardonable, because it is more easily pardoned than the former kind; it does not at once kill the soul, and separate us entirely from God; it is like sickness and not like death, but if it is encouraged it will soon become worse, and end in death: I mean what we call sins of surprise and infirmity, e.g. when persons before they are quite aware give way to their anger and say unkind words: it is a sin, and needs to be repented of and forgiven, but it is not such a sin as fornication, or pride, or malice: a person dying with such a sin upon him, not having distinctly repented of it, would not, we may believe, be of course lost for ever and ever. But even of such sins we cannot be too much afraid; for besides their own badness, no one can tell exactly when they become so much worse as to bring on us the guilt of the other and more fearful sort of sin: and a man may well say to himself, 'What if my indulging in this one liberty, which seems to me not so very bad, should be in the sight of God as if I were putting a kind of seal to my past transgressions? What if it turn the scale against me, when at the last day I shall be judged according to my works?' For fear then of deadly sin I will keep myself as well as I may, through Jesus Christ from lighter and pardonable sin.' That is the only safe way: that is the only true way for us, who pray to Jesus Christ continually, 'from all deadly sin, good Lord, deliver us.'

As the Litany thus teaches us that there is such a thing as deadly sin, sin so bad, that a single deliberate act of it, is enough to kill our souls and cut us off from Christ for ever; so it teaches us at the same time that fornication is such a sin: that is, when people, not being man and wife, come together as man and wife. Whatever may be said of other sins, this surely is deadly sin. Holy Scripture teaches us so expressly, reckoning it among the works of the flesh which are not to be named among Christians: and the Litany, as often as ever we hear it, puts us in mind of the same; puts us in mind that fornication is deadly sin. It is mentioned especially, rather than any other sort of wickedness, perhaps, because very often the temptation to it is so strong, perhaps because too many are inclined to think lightly of it, and pass it over easily, more especially if it be healed (as they imagine) by after marriage. But this is not so at all, brethren; the sin I speak of is so great, that as our blessed Lord Himself assures us, he that doth but allow himself to look with his eyes, and encourage the desire of it in his heart, is, before his

God, guilty of adultery in his heart. Therefore watch: believe the Bible and the Church: believe the great Lord, your Creator and Redeemer, the Maker of heaven, earth, and hell. He surely knows for whom He prepared that aweful place of punishment: He surely knows what sins are deadly, what, in comparison, pardonable : and He plainly tells you that sinful lust, and much more actual uncleanness, is before Him as adultery, and requires, as adultery would, to be healed by very deep and special repentance, before the persons so sinning can be again fit for the kingdom of God. What a pity it would be, should any of those who unhappily have suffered Satan to delude them into sins of this kind, find their mistake too late! What a pity again, nay rather, what a fearful horror, should others coming after, be encouraged by their bad example to make light of such things, and so they should prove a cause of sin to the little ones of Jesus Christ. It were better for them that a millstone were hanged about their neck, and they drowned in the depth of the sea. My dear brethren, my children in Jesus Christ, this is the great, the distressing anxiety of those who have now the care of souls. A notion is gone abroad in the world, that persons turning to God need not trouble themselves to repent so very particularly of their past sins: committed, it may be, many years ago: that we need not confess such sins one by one to God: that it is enough if we feel to our own satisfaction, a certain general change of heart. Now this is right against the doctrine, that certain sins are deadly, and cut off the soul from God: that they leave a bad mark upon us, which must be done away with before we can come to God. It is right against the Bible, which teaches us that the work of godly sorrow by which alone persons can approve themselves to be clear after wilful sin, is a long, a hard, a manifold work. It is right against the Prayerbook, which everywhere teaches that we must be very particular in confessing our sins, our own special sins, one by one if we can, to God: and in very many cases teaches also, that we ought by all means to confess them to him who is over us in God's place. Let there be no mistake in this matter, for indeed it is of the greatest importance. We cannot be forgiven, nor come worthily to the Holy Sacrament, without Christ's absolution: we cannot have Christ's absolution without real sorrow and distinct confession of our own several sins, as distinct as we can make it: confession, I say not, to a Priest, (it may or not be so,) but, to Christ Himself. In this we must exercise ourselves, as ever we hope to be heard, in our prayer to be delivered from fornication and other deadly sin.

Next we pray against a sort of dangers, more subtle, more out of sight, and therefore more dangerous. 'From all the deceits of the world, the flesh, and the devil, good Lord, deliver us.' Not now from their open assaults, from temptation to gross sin, such as fornication: but from their crafts and deceits, the thousand hidden ways in which they steal into our hearts and imaginations, and turn us away from the Truth before we are aware. As for instance, the world says, you must take this or that liberty, since every one else takes it: you must not set up to be so much better than other people, else you will never be able to do them any good. The flesh says, you have denied yourself enough: now is the time to enjoy yourself: you will be forgiven, though you be a little out of order. The devil whispers, 'Another person might be wrong in doing this: but yours is a special case: you have done so many things well, that God will not be angry with you for this one transgression.' These are the deceits of our enemies: from which if we pray to be delivered, we must in all reason watch against them. O, indeed we must watch, and that perseveringly; for these our three enemies are ever at hand, they are ever busy and awake, and we can have no security, except in hiding ourselves under His wings, and asking Him daily and hourly, 'Lord, what wilt Thou have me to do?'

From these prayers against sin, the Church leads us on next to pray against the temporal punishments of sin, such as lightning and tempest; plague, pestilence, and famine; battle and murder, and sudden death. Some of these calamities, you perceive, come suddenly on man, and as it were by strokes, as lightning and tempest: some are wasting and lingering, as plague, pestilence, and famine: and again some of them are brought on man by his fellow men, such as battle and murder; others, as sudden death, are by the immediate visitation of the Almighty. But all of them either come directly from our good God and Father, or are at least allowed and overruled by Him for the punishment of transgressors and for the warning of those who need to be warned: and so we pray against them all: we should be worse than heathens if we did not so pray; to Him Who holds them all in His Hand, even to our Lord Jesus Christ, to Whom is given, as He Himself said, 'all power in heaven and in earth.' Let it be the comfort of those who have seen their friends fall or who fear to fall themselves, under any of these visitations, that none of them can possibly happen: not a sparrow can fall to the ground: without the consent of this our tender Father, Who will lay no more on us than He will make us able to bear: and let those who pray not to die suddenly take care to live so that no death may be quite sudden to them: but that when their Lord shall come and knock (who can tell how soon?) they may open to Him immediately.

But there are worse evils than plague, pestilence, or famine, or any of the rest which can only kill the body: there are evils of the Church, spiritual enough in their effect to destroy thousands both of souls and bodies in hell: storms and tumults which have their beginning, not in God's outward and visible world, but in the restless and unquiet hearts of men. Against these, and their sad ending, we supplicate our Lord once more. 'From all sedition, privy conspiracy, and rebellion; from all false doctrine, heresy, and schism; from hardness of heart, and contempt of Thy Word and commandment, good Lord, deliver us.' Here we see very exactly reckoned up the chief disorders in society, as before in the air and elements. In the State we pray to be delivered from sedition, privy conspiracy, and rebellion: in the Church from false doctrine, heresy, and schism. Three bad things in the State, and three bad things in the Church, in either case going on from bad to worse. In the State sedition, privy conspiracy, and rebellion: sedition, that is, when people allow themselves to dishonour and disobey the king, and those who are in authority under him; privy conspiracy, when they band themselves secretly together, to do something against the law by fraud or by force: rebellion, when they actually lift up their hands against the Lord's anointed, the appointed Governour of the land. And nearly as these sins are in the State, so are false doctrine, heresy, and schism, in the Church. When all come together as too often happens, it is indeed utter confusion. But there are one or two things here, of which I am desirous that we should none of us be utterly ignorant: I mean about false doctrine, heresy, and schism: whereof false doctrine in the Church is like sedition in the State: it infects people, poisons their talk, puts them altogether wrong. And it becomes heresy, when it contradicts the Creed: and the person who holds it is a heretic when he goes on obstinately holding it, after the judgement of the Church has been sufficiently clear against it. And schism, which comes after, is separation from the Apostles' fellowship, as the other was from the Apostles' doctrine. Schism, or cutting off, for so the word means, is when a person cuts himself off from the body that is in communion with the Apostles, i.e. with their successors, the bishops of the Church. How grievous a sin this is, we may judge by its being just contrary to our Lord's last and very earnest prayer just after consecrating the first Eucharist. *He* prayed over and over that we might all be one: but one who goes into schism, one who leaves the Church and chooses a new place for himself, does all he can to keep the Church from uniting: he is therefore working (though he little thinks it) exactly contrary to the Son of God. This is what we beseech God to deliver us from, when we mention false doctrine, heresy, and schism: and believe me, dear brethren, the only safe way for us of this country to receive the blessing we pray for, is to keep faithful, whatever difficulties occur, to our old Prayer-book, to our old Apostolic ministry. That is the way whereby the first Church, the Church of Jerusalem, continued and grew in Christ: God grant it may be our way, and that of all near and dear to us, and of all committed to our charge.

For besides being the right way in itself, it is the way given us, in these trying times, to get over that last and worst evil, hardness of heart, and contempt of God's word and commandment. *That* is the lowest deep of sin in this world, and will lead, we may be sure, to the lowest deep of misery in the other world. 'Hardness of heart,' when the soul wilfully shuts itself up against the voice of God, and the gentle teaching of His Spirit: when it makes itself like the flinty rock, into which the rain of heaven cannot at all sink or penetrate. How can such an one ever be cured, who rejects the only remedy? And then he makes himself too, more and more guilty, for he goes on not in ignorance but in contempt of God's word and commandment. He absolutely scorns and despises the known will of his God and Saviour. Alas! how many are there who do so! how many who are in a way to do so! for every one, brethren, who indulges himself in anything which he knows to be wrong, is surely in the way to this fatal hardness of heart: and as we are continually on the edge of the most fearful *bodily* evils, which are mentioned in the Litany, lightning and tempest, plague, pestilence, and famine, it is but a hair's breadth, for aught we know, between us and the worst of these, and not our wisdom, but God's mercy, keeps them off from us: so is it most alarming to think, how near we have often come, how near we may be now, to these more grievous spiritual evils—rebellion against those who are set over us in the State; false doctrine, heresy, schism in the Church; hardness of heart, and contempt of God's word and commandment. Good Lord, deliver us from these things, and in Thy tender mercy pardon us for having so long and often trifled with them: through Jesus Christ our Lord. Amen.

SERMON V.

ON THE LITANY. V.

HEB. ii. 14, 15.

Forasmuch then as the children are partakers of flesh and blood, He also Himself likewise took part of the same; that through death He might destroy him that had the power of death, that is, the devil; and deliver them who through fear of death were all their lifetime subject to bondage.

IN these words the Apostle sets before us, first, the fact of our Lord's Incarnation, and then the unspeakable benefit freely bestowed upon us thereby.

God the Son, the Second Person in the Holy, Blessed, and Glorious Trinity, made Himself Man, true Man, for us. Forasmuch as the children are partakers of flesh and blood, He also Himself likewise took part of the same. Here is the fact of the Incarnation; next follows the account of the deep eternal blessings which He by becoming Incarnate has provided for us. The Son of God, by being made Man, and by what He did and suffered as Man, delivered us both from the power and the punishment of sin. Through His Death, which He could not have borne but as Man, He destroyed him that had the power of death, i. e. the devil. He overcame him, and thereby freed us from his power, that is, from the *power* of sin. He also delivered us from the *punishment* of sin, i. e. from the death and the fear of it, and from the sad bondage of spirit, the weary and heavy heart, from which they never can be free who know that they must die, and have no hope after death. Thus the Apostle describes the Incarnation and Death of Christ as delivering us from both the power and punishment of sin: as being to us indeed all that we pray for in those earnest petitions in the Litany which we have hitherto been considering. For when we said, ' From sin, from all blindness of heart, from pride, vain-glory and hypocrisy, from envy, hatred, and malice, and all uncharitableness; from all sedition, privy conspiracy, and rebellion, from all false doctrine, heresy, and schism, from hardness of heart, and contempt of God's word and commandment, good Lord, deliver us,' we were praying the Lord to set us free from the power of sin. And when we said, ' From all evil and mischief, from the crafts and assaults of the devil, from Thy wrath and from everlasting damnation; from lightning and tempest, from plague, pestilence, and famine, from battle and murder, and from sudden death, good Lord, deliver us,' then we were asking for deliverance from the *punishment* of sin, temporal and eternal.

And now observe, brethren, on what we are taught to rely, as our only deliverance both from sin and from the misery which sin brings after it. Both by S. Paul here in the Epistle to the Hebrews, and by the Church in her solemn Litany, we are taught to rely, solely and entirely, on the Incarnation of the Son of God, and the chain of mercies whereof that was the first beginning. S. Paul says, He 'took part of flesh and blood, that through death He might destroy the devil, and deliver them that were in bondage.' The Litany says, 'From all these evils: from both the power and the punishment of sin: do Thou, good Lord, deliver us, by the mystery of Thy holy Incarnation, by Thy holy Nativity and Circumcision, by Thy Baptism, Fasting, and Temptation, by Thine Agony and Bloody Sweat, by Thy Cross and Passion, by Thy precious Death and Burial, by Thy glorious Resurrection and Ascension, and by the coming of the Holy Ghost.' Are they not most blessed and comfortable, as well as very noble and heart-cheering words? a true golden chain let down from heaven to earth, yea to the very lowest places and darkest corners of the earth, to draw lost and undone sinners up to the very house of God? And observe, the first link in that chain, that on which all the rest depend, that without which heaven and earth could not really be bound together, is the Incarnation of God the Son. 'By the mystery of Thy holy Incarnation, good Lord, deliver us.' As if we should say, 'We desire, O Lord, to put Thee in mind of all those unspeakable and wonderful mercies, which had their beginning when Thou, the Only-Begotten Son, didst come down to do Thy Father's Will by taking to Thyself a Body and Soul like ours; a true Body formed from her body who was truly one of the seed of Adam : a true Soul breathed into that Body, and like the soul of Adam in all things only without sin. We beseech Thee, for this Thy great mercy's sake, deliver us both from sin and punishment. Remember Thy gracious beginnings towards us, and let them not prove vain and fruitless at last.' Then in like manner we go on to remind our good Lord of all that He did besides, and is doing, as our Mediator. 'By Thy Holy Nativity;' as if we should say, 'Remember how in great humility Thou didst vouchsafe to be born of that poor and humble maiden; remember the stable at Bethlehem, the manger and the swaddling bands: how low, how very low, Thou didst stoop from Thy Throne in heaven ; and for Thy lowliness' sake deliver us.' 'By Thy Circumcision;' i. e. Remember the first bitter taste of pain endured for our sins: let not those precious drops of Thy holy and life-giving Blood be lost, 'by Thy Circumcision: good Lord, deliver us.' 'By thy Baptism :' Remember how at thirty years old Thou didst begin to show Thyself to

Thy people, how Thou didst come to be washed in water by Thy servant, as if Thou hadst been a sinner, Who art purer than the Angels : ' By Thy Baptism, good Lord, deliver us.' ' By Thy fasting : ' Remember the sad and lonely hours, which Thou didst spend in the wilderness, the forty days' hunger and thirst which Thou didst endure ; and for their sake vouchsafe to look compassionately upon us, here in our helpless condition, for we are most helpless if left to ourselves : ' By Thy fasting, good Lord, deliver us.'

' By Thy temptation : ' Thou seest how hard we are beset, how our great adversary walketh about, seeking every moment to devour us: what fatal advantage he finds against us in the evil example of others and in our own frail hearts : O leave us not to him, nor to the world, nor to ourselves; for Thine own sufferings' sake when Thou didst vouchsafe to be in all points tempted as we are, succour us when we are tempted: ' By Thy temptation, good Lord, deliver us.'

' By Thine Agony and bloody Sweat.' Remember how Thou didst withdraw Thyself from Thy disciples : how Thou didst kneel upon the cold hard ground: how Thou didst fall flat upon Thy face, and pray earnestly, again and again : how Thy divine Soul was as it were torn in pieces, willing at the same moment and not willing to receive the bitter cup: how in the agony and struggle of that prayer Thy Sweat was as it were great drops of blood falling down to the ground: O Lord, remember all this for the good of us Thy unworthy servants and of those for whom we pray: and suffer not Thy unspeakable pangs to be void and fruitless in our behalf by reason of our many and most inexcusable transgressions. 'By Thine Agony and bloody Sweat, good Lord, deliver us.'

'By thy Cross and Passion.' As in all our prayers and addresses to the Father of all we plead the Sufferings and Death of the Son as our only available Sacrifice and sin-offering, so here we plead with the Son Himself by the remembrance of the same Sacrifice: as if a man should say to his friend who had done and suffered great things for him, 'Remember thine old loving-kindness, and help me once more, unworthy as I am, else all that former friendship will fall to the ground and be as if it had never been. Thus do we Christians plead with the Saviour by His Cross, and because He has redeemed us, we beseech Him to spare us; or as Moses pleaded with God for the Israelites when he had brought them out of Egypt, that He should not cast them off, because it would be a triumph to His enemies the Egyptians and Canaanites, so we cry out, 'Lest the enemy say, I have prevailed against him,' lest Thy Blood be counted an unholy thing, 'By Thy Cross and Passion, good Lord, deliver us.'

On the Litany. V.

Then we plead with Him by His precious Death and Burial: because we are going to ask His mercy in our own death especially: as if we should say, 'Thou knowest what death is: none of us who are living know; it is a mystery alike to the child and to the aged, to the wise man and the fool: but Thou knowest by actual suffering as we shall one day know: and that suffering so endured for us, that it was as it were all the deaths of us sinners in one. Remember those bitter pangs, we beseech Thee, and because of them have mercy upon us in the dreadful hour of death to which we are doomed: help us to prepare for it and support us when we come to it: By Thy precious Death and Burial, good Lord, deliver us.' We put Him in mind of His Burial as well as of His Death, because that too was part of His humiliation : and even because He once lay in the grave, we pray Him to watch over us when we shall be laid in our graves, and to keep our bodies safe against the Day of resurrection: 'By Thy Burial, good Lord, deliver us.'

And with that we pass from His sufferings to His triumph, from His humiliation to His glory: and we plead with Him by His glorious Resurrection and Ascension: as who should say, 'The Lord hath delivered Thee, the pangs of Thy death have been loosed, Thou Who art the Head hast been lifted up far above all heavens: now then it is meet that Thou draw up Thy members after Thee. Thou sittest at the Right Hand of God in the glory of the Father: we believe that Thou shalt come to be our Judge: we therefore pray Thee, help Thy servants whom Thou hast redeemed with Thy precious Blood; By Thy glorious Resurrection and Ascension, good Lord, deliver us.'

And finally we plead with our Lord by that which is the crown of all His mercies to man, even the sending down His Holy Spirit. I call it the crown of all His mercies, because it is that by which He applies all, and brings them all, as it were, home to us. 'By the coming of the Holy Ghost, good Lord, deliver us:' i.e. seeing that Thou didst vouchsafe according to Thy promise to send to Thy faithful people after Thy departure Thine own Co-equal Spirit to be their Comforter, and to give us in Holy Baptism our portion of the same Spirit; remember this Thy mercy most especially in our behalf, and let it not be lost upon us: for Thine own sake continue it to us, O Lord, and suffer us not to cast it away: let us not sin against the Holy Spirit. 'By His coming, His gracious coming to the whole Church at Pentecost, His coming to each one of us in His Holy Sacraments, again we pray, good Lord, deliver us.'

There is yet another meaning, another thought, which runs as a thread through all this part of the

Litany : viz. that when we say to our Lord, 'By the mystery of Thy holy Incarnation, By Thine Agony and bloody Sweat,' and all those other petitions, we mean to pray that each one of the great mysterious things which He did and suffered for us may do its proper work, and tell towards bringing about the salvation of us sinners, as He graciously designed. For so it is, brethren, that in all that course of wonders, from His Conception in His Mother's womb to His sending down the Comforter on His Apostles, He had each one of us in mind: we, even you and I, and every one here present, were so much in His mind, as if there had been no one besides to be saved or lost. Here then we pray for ourselves and for one another, that what He then did and suffered for us may not be frustrated by our manifold faults. For thus it is: Before the world began, He knew and purposed in His Divine Wisdom that such and such persons should be: that they, by their own sins and the sins of their forefathers being in danger of eternal death, He, in His own good time, would come down from heaven for their salvation, and would be incarnate by the Holy Ghost of the Virgin Mary, and would be made Man, and would suffer death for them, and would rise again, and ascend into heaven, and send down the Holy Ghost. And in all this chain of mercies, observe, the first link is the Incarnation, i.e. His being made Man.

He could not die and suffer for us, unless He had a Body and Soul like ours: for death is the parting of body and soul: He could not be a perfect Priest and Sacrifice, unless He were in all things made like unto His brethren, only without sin. His Burial and Rising again, and Ascending into heaven, were all in the Body, and so, in some way, was His sitting at the Right Hand of God. And the very purpose of His sending the Holy Ghost was to make us sacramentally partakers of His spiritual Body, that so we might be joined to His mystical Body, the Church. So that even according to our weak understanding, all depends on the true and real Incarnation of the Son of God. *That* is the Foundation: everything depends upon it. *That* is the one Truth, by which we are to judge and try all other doctrines that are preached to us. ' ᵃ Every spirit that confesseth that Jesus Christ is come in the flesh is 'of God: and every spirit that confesseth not that Jesus Christ is come in the flesh is not of God: and this is that spirit of Anti-christ, whereof ye have heard that it should come, and even now already is it in the world.'

But, my dear brethren, we must not go away, without some serious thought of the various times in which the Church teaches us to call for the help of this our Incarnate Saviour. 'In all time of our

ᵃ 1 S. John iv. 2, 3.

tribulation, in all time of our wealth;' tribulation, i.e. trouble and sorrow; and wealth, i.e. (here) prosperity and success, take in between them all possible conditions, all possible events in the world: but perhaps the prayer is more especially meant to ask the aid of God Incarnate, i.e. of our Lord Jesus Christ, in times of more than usual distress, and also in times of more than usual joy. The first of these we understand very well: it is the most obvious of all things, it is what all but unbelievers practise, to call upon the Lord in time of trouble: but why should we so especially cry out, 'Good Lord, deliver us,' in times of wealth and enjoyment, and when all seems going well with us? Our Lord Himself will presently help us to an answer. '[b] Woe unto you that are rich, for ye have received your consolation:' and 'it is easier for a camel to go through a needle's eye, than for a rich man to enter into the kingdom of God.' Because the snares of Satan are so very crafty and the temptations of the world so very alluring, when a man by his wealth has power in a great measure to please himself. Let us pray, then, brethren, with all our might, 'In all time of our wealth, good Lord, deliver us:' and as we pray, so let us watch: whenever God sends any special joy or blessing, yea even if it be spiritual joy and comfort, let us watch and stand on our guard, that neither we

[b] S. Luke vi. 24.

in our frailty, nor the enemy in his malice, pervert the good gift into an occasion of offending. Let us ever pray and strive that our satisfactions and prosperities may have in them a touch of what is humiliating, and chastening: even as our Redeemer won His victory for us no other way but by His Cross and Passion.

Yet once more: we pray also, and it is the last prayer in this part of the Litany, that our Lord would deliver us from all the evils which have been mentioned, in the hour of death more especially, and in the day of judgement. For we know not whether or no our time to come will be a time of wealth or of tribulation: but whichever it be, we know for certain that it will end in death and judgement: and that in death and judgement there can be no hope, no rest, no comfort, no help, but only in Christ our Lord: Who will surely be there, if not to deliver, to condemn us. O then how can we help praying as we do here in the Litany? how can we help calling night and day on our gracious God, Incarnate to be our Saviour, and with all our might beseeching Him to own us on that great and dreadful Day? Be sure, He loves to be so prayed to: He made Himself Bone of our bone and Flesh of our flesh, He sacrificed Himself for us, He gives Himself to us in His Sacraments, that we may pray to Him in earnest. Do so, my brethren; pray to Him and live to Him, in earnest: and be sure He will not forsake His own work. The mystery of His holy Incarnation, which is your only hope now, will be your stay in death and judgement, and after judgement will prove to you an exceeding and eternal weight of glory.

SERMON VI.

ON THE LITANY. VI.

THE INTERCESSIONS.

1 TIM. ii. 1, 2.

I exhort therefore, that, first of all, supplications, prayers, intercessions, and giving of thanks, be made for all men; for kings, and for all that are in authority; that we may lead a quiet and peaceable life in all godliness and honesty.

WE have now finished that part of the Litany, in which the Church calls upon her Lord to deliver us from all evils, both of this world and of the next: reminding Him at the same time of His great unspeakable mercies, from His Incarnation to His sending down the Holy Ghost. And now we go on to pray and intercede with Him to bestow upon us all good. The first petition being that He would rule and govern His holy Church universal in the right way: the last, that He would 'give us true repentance, forgive us all our sins, negligences, and ignorances, and endue us with the grace of the Holy Spirit, to amend our lives according to His holy Word.' And after each petition the congregation are to make answer, as you know,

'We beseech Thee to hear us, good Lord.' There are twenty-two short prayers of this kind, and when we consider them, we shall find, I think, that the first ten are petitions for public blessings, blessings which we need as belonging to the kingdom or people in which God has cast our lot: and in the other twelve we ask Him for things which we or others need each one for himself. They are for the most part prayers of intercession, that is to say, we pray in them for other people as much or more than for ourselves. And this is a great part of Christian charity: to speak a good word for one another, as often and as earnestly as we can, to the everlasting Father, in the Name of our Lord; or, as in the Litany, to our gracious Lord Himself. Even as He by His Apostle ordains in the text. For in those verses which I read to you for the text, S. Paul is giving directions to Timothy, whom he had ordained to be a Bishop, how he should order the public prayers of the Church. And he exhorts, first of all, that prayers and thanksgivings be made for Christians to use in common, not each one for himself only, nor in their families only, but in the Church and congregation, when we meet to offer to God His own memorial Sacrifice of His Son's Body and Blood. At such times, S. Paul directs that prayers should be made for all men, especially for kings and all who are in authority. Accordingly we find that the first good thing which we beseech God in the Litany to grant us, after we have prayed for deliverance from all evil things, is His ruling and governing the Church in the right way. And observe, we say the Church universal: the whole body of Christians everywhere. They are His Body, having His Spirit breathed into them: even as at the beginning He breathed into Adam's nostrils the breath of life: and He hath promised the same Spirit to guide them into all truth: so that we are sure that the holy Church Universal, i. e. the Church of all times and all nations, will not err, will not go wrong; as it is written, 'a My Spirit which I have given thee, and My words which I have put into thy mouth, shall not depart out of thy mouth, nor out of the mouth of thy seed, nor out of the mouth of thy seed's seed, saith the Lord, from henceforth even for ever.' A particular nation, or a particular generation of the Church, may perhaps err, and that grievously, but not the whole Church from the Apostles until now: and therefore we are sure that the Creeds are all right, and also all the chief parts of the Prayer-book: because they are what has been taught and practised, as the true meaning of the Bible, in the whole Church from the Apostles until now. Well then, in this first intercession of the Litany we do as it were put our Lord in mind of His gracious and bountiful promises to this His Holy Church, and

* Isa. lix. 21.

beseech Him that He would never suffer it in any generation to fall away from the faith and practice of the saints; and especially not in our generation, nor for our sins, as we have too much reason to fear. We beseech Him as sinners: not for our own righteousness, but for His manifold and great mercies: and unworthy as we are, He permits us to take comfort in the great things which He has done for other generations of sinners within His Church. Ten thousand times, we may well fear, have both our fathers and we forfeited all right to this His merciful protection: but He 'ᵇ hath delivered us from so great a death, and doth deliver; and we trust in Him that He will also yet deliver us:' but He expects that we should all help together with our prayers. Pray then, brethren, pray more and more earnestly, for the Church of God, now in her time of trial. She is always in warfare, but never more so than now. Pray night and morning for the whole body of Christ, your brethren in every Christian land far and near: pray humbly, pray earnestly, pray with a heart set against sin, and your prayer will return into your own bosom; whether you see any fruit of it in the conversion and improvement of the world or no, the God of love and peace, will surely bless it to the improvement of your own heart in peace and love.

ᵇ 2 Cor. i. 10.

And for the same kind of reason which would make you pray very devoutly for the whole Church, you will be serious and devout also in the following petitions of the Litany, in which we proceed, according to the Apostle's direction, to make intercession for our Sovereign and for all who are in authority. You may easily understand why the Church prays so often for the king or queen of the land, remembering them in all her solemn services. The Sovereign is over us in the place of God, and has to bear the burden of the whole state: he is the person of most consequence, the wellbeing of the nation chiefly depends upon him: he is also in a place of great danger and temptation, and we are too apt through the stubbornness and wilfulness of our nature, to forget our duty to him in one respect or another. All these are reasons for our often and cheerfully remembering the king or queen in our prayers. S. Paul and the first Christians never omitted to pray for the Roman emperor, though he was always a heathen, and very often a cruel tyrant: let us all try at least to be in earnest when we pray for our Christian queen, for indeed her place is as hard as it is high, and she needs all the help her loving subjects can obtain for her from the King of kings. Who would not pray with all his heart that she may be kept and strengthened in God's true worship, i.e. the faith and practice of the Prayerbook to which she is so many ways pledged, but in which whoever is earnest, and most especially in such a high place, must expect to find many hindrances? Who would not pray that she may be kept in righteousness and holiness of life, so hard to be practised by the rich and great ones of the earth? Who would not pray that her heart may be ordered in the faith, fear, and love of God? that she may evermore have affiance and trust, not in her great and rich dominions, but in Him? that she may ever seek, not any thing in this world, but always His honour and glory? Who would not pray that the Allmerciful would continue to be as He has hitherto proved in a remarkable manner, her defender and keeper, giving her the victory over all her enemies, and especially over all those evil men and evil spirits, who are her worst enemies, because they are also the enemies of God and His Church? And as we pray for her, so in dutifulness we pray for those who are nearest to her, as being in many respects partakers of her burthen, and in their example, of great consequence to us.

After interceding for our chief governour in the state, we proceed to mention our spiritual fathers and governours the Bishops, Priests, and Deacons; those to whom God has given His Spirit to be over us in holy things. We beseech Him to illuminate them with true knowledge and understanding of His Word, that is of the Bible according to its real meaning, taught to the

Church from the beginning. Take notice of this, brethren: we pray to be taught, not simply the Bible, but the true meaning of the Bible. And another thing: you pray that we may teach it you, not by word only but by example, not only by preaching but by living. For if we say and do not; if we lay heavy burthens on you, and ourselves touch not the burthens with one of our fingers; if we show others the way of goodness, ourselves going on in impurity and falseness of heart: who can express the greatness of our misery? Of your charity then pray for us, that we may be saved from this worst and most shameful of all miscarriages: that we may not be found at last such as Judas Iscariot: cast away ourselves, after preaching to others. Pray for us, that we may preach faithfully, and that as we may preach, so we may live: that it may not be said to us at the Day of Judgement, 'out of thine own mouth will I judge thee, thou wicked servant.' And as we pray for our queen by name, so it may seem natural that in our hearts, even though not in our lips, we should name our own bishop and the priest or other minister who has the care of our souls. May we not hope that many do so both here in the Litany, and at home when you are praying for those whom Christ would have you pray for? Certainly, in such measure as the ministers of Christ are in earnest, it will be a real comfort to them in their anxious duties to know that you, the sheep of Christ, pray earnestly and particularly for them. It ought to help us very much in our duties towards one another, our being in the habit of praying one for another.

After the Clergy we pray for the nobility, and all the counsellors of the Sovereign, that God would endue them with grace, wisdom, and understanding: and then for the magistrates, that they may have grace to execute justice on criminals, and maintain truth in disputes and lawsuits. Thus we call down the blessing of Him Who is the Perfection of wisdom and justice, both on those who advise the king or queen what to do, what laws to make: and on those whose duty it is to enforce and fulfil the law after it is made. We pray for them, and of course it is our duty to do nothing which may hinder them in their good work; to judge them charitably, and speak respectfully of them.

The prayers for all sorts of governours being finished, a petition for the Christian people comes next in order: 'That it may please Thee to bless and keep all Thy people.' *Thy people:* i.e. Christ's people, especially those who belong to the particular congregation which is saying the Litany: and here again each person will naturally and rightly remember his own special kindred, friends, and neighbours: those for whom he is bound to pray.

The last petition on which I shall say anything

to-day, is that in which the Church teaches us to remember other nations besides our own, and to pray that God would give them unity, peace, and concord. He is the God of peace: He came to be our Peace: the Angels at His coming sang 'Peace on earth:' yet it is a sad truth, that not only the heathens and unbelievers, who refuse in all things to hearken to His voice, but Christian nations, made up of members of Christ, have been, some or other of them, almost always at war with one another: and what is still a deeper ground of sadness, Christian Churches are divided one from another. When the Church first begun, it was not only one Church all over the world, but it was plainly seen to be one Church, in that everywhere they received Christians coming from another country into Communion: but now there are sad divisions: if we go across the sea we find whole nations of Christians, not willing to communicate with us, nor to receive us into their Communion. It need not disturb any one, for it is only what our Saviour prophesied: but it is very sad, and very hurtful, and very contrary to His Will, being in fact altogether occasioned by the manifold sins of Christians: and therefore we do well to pray with all earnestness that this great evil may be remedied: that there may not only be peace among Christian nations, but unity also and concord,—visible unity and concord —among Christian Churches. It is one of our most solemn prayers, both here in the Litany and afterwards in the Communion office: as our Lord Himself offered it up the night before His Death along with His first Sacrifice of Communion: 'I pray that they all may be one, as We are.' When we think of that prayer, brethren, how can we help offering up with all our hearts, the petition for unity and concord, seeing that the wish for it was so very near the Heart of our pierced and dying Lord? If we at all love Him, if we at all care for Him, let us sincerely watch ourselves, that we do nothing, say nothing, if possible think nothing, which may tend to divide and scatter the Church: as for instance, if a preacher not of the Church should come here, or if any of you should be called by God's providence to live in a place where you were tempted to attend such preaching, it is your plain duty to know no such thing as doubt or unbelief in the matter, but to decline all such preaching as contrary to His Will.

In this respect, as in respect of the other petitions which have been considered to-day, the poorest, the humblest, the most ignorant, may do great things if he will. He may say to himself '*I* do great things! I who am so weak, so simple?' 'Yes,' Christ says to him, '*You* may, if you will, be of great service to the king, the bishops, the nobles, to the divided Church, if you will but pray earnestly and worthily.' The poor widow, the lonely orphan, praying patiently may do great things for the Church. Remember Cornelius and how his private prayer was answered. God is the same God as He was then. He will hear you as He did Cornelius, if you try to be like Cornelius. Your quiet prayer and self-denial in secret may go farther than you imagine to restore that greatest blessing, the unity and concord of the Church.

SERMON VII.

ON THE LITANY. VII.

THE PRIVATE INTERCESSIONS.

HEB. xiii. 18.

Pray for us: for we trust we have a good conscience, in all things willing to live honestly.

AFTER our intercessions for public persons, our mother the Church helps us to pray for private and individual Christians, i.e. for ourselves and for one another and for those who need to be prayed for all over the world, according to their several circumstances and wants. I say, the Church our mother thus helps us to pray: for this is the way in which I should like that we should all use ourselves to look at the Prayer-book, viz. as though we were little children kneeling at our mother's knees to learn how to pray, and she was teaching us, as of course all good and religious mothers do teach their children. When we are willing simply to learn of her, and to pray in such words, and in such a spirit, as she approves, then we are in the right way of prayer, then we are sure of not going away from our prayers without a blessing. And now in the particular part of the Litany we are come to, the Church in her wisdom and charity instructs us, to offer up our prayers for the souls and bodies of our brethren, as well as our own, according as every man hath need. We may understand it as if the whole congregation of Christ's flock called on us in the words used by the Apostle in the text: 'Pray for us: for we trust we have a good conscience, in all things willing to live honestly.' We pray for all, but especially for those who are of the household of Faith; those who have a sort of good meaning : who have not quite given themselves up to hardness of heart and contempt of God's Word and commandment. They wish to live honestly in all things, and we pray for them that they may be helped to do so.

And the first thing we ask is, that they and we, and each one of us, may walk in the fear and obedience of Christ. 'That it may please Thee to give us a heart to love and dread Thee, and diligently to live after Thy commandments.' Not only to love, but also to dread and fear Him : not only to dread, but also to love Him. And that because He is our Father, and a dutiful child both honours and respects his father, i. e. has a religious fear and dread of doing anything which may displease him: and also loves him very dearly, and therefore is most earnest in doing all things to please him: according to the end of this petition. Where there is true love and fear, there is also the living diligently after His commandments: after *all* of them; dutiful children do not pick and choose which of their Father's sayings they will mind and which they will not mind, but they live diligently after them all. And this we ask for every one alike, for to every one it is alike needful. It is absolutely necessary: no man can be saved without it. I mean, it is absolutely necessary that we should be so far turned to God, as to have a heart, i.e. a mind and purpose: not merely an unsteady wish, coming and going, and blown about by every wind of temptation, but a real, settled, mind and purpose, to love and fear God, and live by His law, in all things. This, I suppose, is what our Saviour meant, when He said to that young man, 'If thou wilt enter into life, keep the commandments:' that it should at least be the rule of his life to do so, and that if ever he turned from it, it should be by infirmity, not of set and deliberate purpose. And then, as our Lord went on and added what may be called Counsels to necessary commands; saying first by way of command, 'If thou wilt enter into life, keep the commandments,' and afterwards by way of counsel, 'If thou wilt be perfect, sell all that thou hast, and give to the poor;' so the Church after praying for a heart to

love and fear and obey God, goes on and prays for
increase of grace: that we may abound more and
more, not only doing those things which not to do
would be deadly sin, but from day to day hearing God's
Word, and receiving it with pure affection, and bringing forth the fruits of the Spirit. See, brethren, what
you pledge yourselves to when in answer to this
petition you say, 'We beseech Thee to hear us, good
Lord.' You do in effect promise to hear God's Word
meekly: i.e. with a sweet, affectionate, teachable mind:
not fretting nor being angry when you feel yourselves
reproved by it: like David and not like Pharaoh or
Jeroboam. You promise to receive it with pure affection: i.e. with a single and simple purpose to please
Him and not yourselves. You promise to bring forth
the fruits of the Spirit, i.e. really to do, on occasion,
the things which God's Word tells you that you ought
to do. I say, you *promise* all this: for in praying for
grace to do it, you surely pledge yourself to do what in
you lies towards it: just as if you asked for seed to sow
a field, the person giving you the seed would understand that you promised to sow it. Take care then,
you who come here and say the Litany, that you
listen to God's Word, that you let it sink into your
hearts, above all, that you obey it in your lives: else
you condemn yourselves, every time you say this
petition.

On the Litany. VII.

After thus praying for all Christians, first that they may be good, then that they may go on better and better, we proceed to pray for different sorts of persons, who more particularly need our prayers, and first, for all such as have erred and are deceived, that they may be led into the way of truth. This is what the Church would have us do with regard to all who are in error, she would have us pray for them, even as we pray for ourselves. And great need there is that we should do so: more and more need, as the world grows older and older, and divisions and heresies grow, alas! more common among Christians. We in our blindness are too apt to dislike those who differ from us, but the Church's way is to teach us to pray for them; and in doing so we pray for ourselves also, in whatever respect we ourselves are deceived, and in error about the things of God: for of course we cannot suppose that *we* are *exactly* right in everything, though we trust that by His mercy we are not in fatal error. Well, whatever our errors and mistakes, as concerning holy things, may be, we here pray against them: humbly claiming the gracious promise of our Lord to all His people, 'when He, the Spirit of truth, shall come, He will guide you into all truth.'

And next, the Church will have us remember the different spiritual conditions of our brethren that are in the world: all tempted, all in danger, all by nature children of wrath, and carrying about with them the seeds at least and deadly infection of original sin; but in very different stages of the way towards heaven: some remaining in that happy state to which they were admitted by holy Baptism: keeping their first love, their garments yet pure and undefiled: and concerning these we pray our good Lord, that it may please Him to 'strengthen such as do stand.' For as we need His special grace to be converted and regenerated at first, so we need it no less for our continuance but for one hour in the grace of our regeneration and union with Christ. He is not only our Creator but our Preserver. Perseverance, the crown of all Christian graces, must come from Him: and who that knows the misery of backsliding and falling away will not pray with all his heart to be kept firm and constant, both himself and all whom he prays for? Or if any be shaken and unsettled, will he not in charity pray for them too, saying as the Church next teaches, 'That it may please Thee to comfort and help the weak-hearted?' Surely, whether it be in matters of faith or of practice, there is nothing more miserable, there are few things more likely to give occasion to the crafts and assaults of the devil, than to be put in doubt, to be hesitating and perplexed about things which one had seemed to one's self clearly to know. It was indeed the Evil one's first step in tempting Eve: '*Hath* God said?'

he wanted to make her *doubt*, whether God had forbidden that particular fruit to them, or no. And there is another hesitation and weakness of heart, even worse than this of doubt : i. e. when persons knowing their duty for certain, have not the heart, the courage, the spirit, to do it. Pilate for instance was weak-hearted when he gave up our Lord in order to content the people: and Saul was very weak-hearted, when for the same reason he spared the choice of the Amalekites. We have great need to ask God for comfort and help against *this* weakness of heart, which would lead us every day to give up our plainest duties, and in the end to throw away our souls, out of mere cowardice—fear of pain or ridicule.

Next, as it is more miserable to sink down than merely to tremble, we say, 'That it may please Thee to raise up them that fall,' them that fall into sin, be the sin ever so great and deadly. Here, as in all these petitions, we shall naturally each one of us remember those persons for whom we are especially bound to pray, those among our own acquaintance or kindred, or with whom we are any way entrusted, who are unhappily living in any serious sin. They cannot be named aloud to be prayed for, as the afflicted sometimes are. It is therefore the more necessary that we should of our own accord call them to mind: that we should beseech God to grant them in particular the benefit of the prayers of the Universal Church. We must pray for them the rather, on account of their never praying for themselves. And who knows what good it might do them: how many poor lost souls might be won back from Satan, if sincere persons would only be thoughtful and constant in praying for them that fall?

Suppose then these three sorts prayed for: the fallen, the wavering, and such as do stand, and God to hear our prayers for each: you see that the next petition would at once be fulfilled. Satan would be beaten or bruised under our feet, and as often as he tried to raise himself up, he would be thrust down again as by the strong spear of an Angel: till at length all God's faithful servants would be taken for ever out of Satan's reach: out of temptation and danger; out of this world.

From spiritual and invisible troubles we pass to the earthly and temporal miseries by which God tries us, and we mention one by one the classes of persons, whom we suppose to be most helpless, most in need of God's very special care, because there is no one on earth who knows how to help them. In general, all in danger, necessity, tribulation: in particular, all travelling by land or by water: and among these we shall ever do well to remember those who are gone out, as zealous preachers and missionaries, to make known the Gospel in the four corners of the earth. Again we pray for all women labouring of child: for such an one, too, is both in great pain and peril and also very much hindered from regular services and devotions of her own. For the same reasons we make mention of sick persons and young children: the more *their own* prayers are hindered, the more active must be *our* intercession. Think too of the many casualties to which young children are especially exposed: so that the two first years after birth are beyond comparison the most dangerous and difficult years for a person to get through: and join with all your heart in the touching prayer for those little ones: which before now, I doubt not, has been many a broken-hearted parent's comfort. And be not inattentive to the next clause, which mentions all prisoners and captives: considering what a rest and relief it would be to you, were you yourself in prison and captivity, to know that the whole Church of God and especially your friends and relations at home, were calling upon the great Deliverer for you: after the pattern of that first Church which when Peter was kept in prison, made prayer unto God for him, and that without ceasing.

As for the next petition, for 'the fatherless children and widows, and for those that are desolate and oppressed,' I need not say much of it: it tells its own meaning plainly, and who can doubt that it is a petition most acceptable to Him Who proclaims Himself a Father of the fatherless and an Avenger of the cause of the widows? And observe that it adds, 'all that are desolate and oppressed:' all that are forlorn in heart and circumstances, though they be not exactly fatherless children or widows. O what tender, considerate love is here: what support for the sufferer, what deep reproof for the oppressor! Who would not love that holy Church, and pray for her in her wrongs, when she is oppressed by ungodly and undutiful men; she who pleads thus earnestly for all that are oppressed before her God?

In the next sentence she spreads her wings as it were, to gather under them this whole world of sinners: beseeching the God of all to have mercy upon all. And in the next after, she causes us to pray—let us take care that we pray in earnest: for those whom men would be least inclined to mention in their prayers, were God Almighty to leave them to themselves; i.e. for 'our enemies, persecutors, and slanderers.' These two petitions between them are as wide as Christian charity, showing that nobody can be so far from us, nor yet so much our enemy, as that we ought not to love them and pray for them, and if we can, do them good: even as our Lord died for all, and in dying prayed especially for His murderers. They show also, as He in that prayer, that we should never despair of anyone.

After all these intercessions for others and prayers for spiritual good, comes in one short Prayer for the • things needful to our temporal and earthly life. 'That it may please Thee to give and preserve to our use the kindly fruits of the earth, so as in due time we may enjoy them.' Whereby we are taught the same lesson as in the Lord's Prayer: 'Give us this day our daily bread:' which words, not coming in till we are half way through the prayer, show us that we are not to make so very much of the good things of this world, in comparison of the better things of heaven. At the same time we are instructed to depend not on our own skill and industry, but on the blessing of our Creator both for the growth and preservation of the fruits of the earth, and for our enjoyment of them.

But what is this which comes in at the end of all? 'That it may please Thee to give us true repentance:' as much as to say, 'We have made bold to ask of Thee all these things, but too well do we know how unworthy we are to ask Thee for anything at all.' When we have done our prayers, we have need to begin again with a prayer that we may pray better: and we have much cause to repent of our very repentance. But Thou, O Lord, have mercy upon us and accept of our most imperfect services; and grant that all our life hereafter may be an exercise of true repentance, Thou forgiving us and we amending our lives. Forgive us what we have done ignorantly, what we have left undone negligently, and especially forgive us our known and wilful sins: and grant that the time to come may be really better, far better than the time past. May Thy Word and Will be henceforth the rule of our lives: and for the rest, 'Thy Will be done.'

And so end the petitions and intercessions of our solemn Litany. We have used it, some of us regularly for many years. God forgive us that we are not very much more improved and bettered by it than we now are. God give His grace to those who are to come after, and to ourselves in future years, that the fruit of our prayers may appear in our lives, and that both our lives and our prayers may prepare us for a blessing hereafter, through Jesus Christ our Lord.

SERMON VIII.

ON THE LITANY. VIII.

THE SUFFRAGES.

Heb. vii. 25.

He is able to save them to the uttermost that come unto God by Him, seeing He ever liveth to make intercession for them.

YES, my brethren: even 'to the uttermost.' There is no evil from which we may not hope to be delivered, there is no degree of joy and mercy, at which we may not hope to arrive, by the mercy of Him on Whom we call in the Litany: Him Who redeemed us with His precious Blood, Who gave Himself for us, once for all, on the Cross, and is daily giving Himself to us in His holy Sacraments. On Him we must call, to keep us safe in ordinary times; to Him we must cry aloud, and run for shelter, when the worst comes to the worst: in all the storms and tempests, and sore trials and troubles, which are sure to come upon us all, more or less, sooner or later.

The Litany, and especially this latter portion of it, to which we are now come, seems especially intended to help us in the worst of times, and most especially of all, perhaps, when the times are bad in respect of God's Holy Church: as we shall see by examining the words of it more particularly.

The point in the Litany at which we began this afternoon in our catechizing, was the end of what are called the Suffrages, or special petitions, the last 'we beseech Thee to hear us, good Lord.' Having in those special petitions besought our Lord to hear us concerning all the sorts of blessings, spiritual and temporal, which we may hope for at His merciful hands, and also for all the persons on whose behalf we are bound to pray: having prayed for each severally: we now proceed to gather up all in certain short addresses and calls on our Blessed Lord, in some respects not unlike the cries of an infant to its parent, cries not expressed in words, yet truly signifying the wants and distresses of the child, and so understood by the parent. Not unlike to these in some respects are the short ejaculations, 'Son of God, we beseech Thee to hear us;' and the others which follow it, wherein both Priest and people take part. Rightly used, those short prayers are a kind of darts kindled by adoring love, and sure not to miss their aim; sure to reach the heart of Him to Whom they are directed, if we do but direct them towards Him in spirit and in truth: if we do but say the words sincerely, earnestly, humbly. The time is very short, which we have for so lifting up our hearts: 'Son of God, we beseech Thee to hear us;' and 'O Christ, hear us,' take up but a moment in uttering: but who knows how great things may be done in that moment, if we really endeavour to throw our whole heart and soul into the words so uttered? To be born, to die, to rise again; to be baptized, confirmed, ordained, to receive Holy Communion, are things done each in a moment, or a very few moments: but how infinitely important are they to be well or ill done: and so it may be, that if Christians would really join, with serious, clean, and prepared hearts, in such brief prayers as these, blessings beyond thought would be won in a few moments, which are now lost, perhaps for ever, for want of such diligence in prayer. You might think perhaps that these prayers must be easy to offer, because the words are so short, few, and plain; but do you find it so yourselves, my brethren? Is it, or is it not, easy for you to say *with all your hearts*, 'Son of God, we beseech Thee to hear us,' or 'O Christ, hear us?' No, it is not easy, nor common for persons to pray these prayers in earnest, for it is both a hard and an unusual thing for any of us truly and really to feel with all our hearts that we are speaking to the Son of God, to Jesus Christ, really present, really close to us, really hearing and listening to what we say, really seeing and marking which way our thoughts are turned: it is a hard and rare thing to feel this, and to call upon Him accordingly, with all our heart, soul, and strength, as a drowning man would call for aid to a friend standing on the shore; as S. Peter called to Jesus when he found himself beginning to sink; as an infant in distress calls on its mother or its nurse. Depend upon it, by the time you have got to be quite in earnest in these calls to Christ in the Litany, you will have made, by God's mercy, no small step in the spiritual life. But now let us see what the titles are, whereby the Church teaches us to address our Saviour in these our childlike outcries to Him. The first is Son of God: before, in the Litany, it had been God the Son, and Good Lord: now it is Son of God: as though we should say, 'we call upon Thee, as on that Man, Who is also God, the Only-begotten of the Father: hear us and plead for us with Thy Father.' Again the priest teaching us to call Him, as S. John the Baptist did long ago, 'The Lamb of God that takest away the sins of the world,' we answer first, 'Have mercy upon us,' and then 'Grant us Thy peace:' meaning that both from Him and through Him only can we have either mercy for past sins or the peace of the Lord to help us on our heavenly way: and not only meaning and believing that it is so, but earnestly speaking to Christ as present, and praying Him that so it may be with us. How many of us, my brethren, who joined in the Litany this morning, did at these words really in his heart ask Christ for pardon and peace?

But observe what follows next. The Church, under the shadow as it were of our Lord's protecting wings, leads us to the very throne of the Most High God, and instructs us how to bring our cause before Him. All the Three Persons are called upon in order: the Incarnate Son presents us in a manner to the Holy, Blessed, and Glorious Trinity. Thus once again are we solemnly taught that He is our only Mediator and Advocate: there is no approaching God but through Christ. But being introduced by His gracious favour, we go on and say to the Father the prayer which Christ Himself taught us. We say the Lord's Prayer: *that* of course is a necessary part of every Christian Litany: and we say it, here perhaps most especially, in our Saviour's sense and not in our own. Consider a little while what this comes to. It is likely that in using any good prayer we who do but use it would fall far short of the meaning of him who composed the prayer. We might think much and cleverly, but we should not think exactly as he did. How much more, when we reflect Who was the real Author of this prayer: even the Most High God, the Searcher of hearts, Who only knoweth what is in man. Therefore it is well that on joining here in the Lord's Prayer we should strive to remember that it is Christ praying for us, not so much we praying for ourselves: and accordingly throughout the prayer we may submit ourselves to Him and to the Father in this way: 'Our Father which art in heaven; high over us as heaven over earth, and in wisdom and love infinitely more in regard to us than the dearest of earthly parents to his offspring: Hallowed be Thy Name; we know not how, but in such ways as Thou knowest to be best: Thy kingdom come; though we be brought very low: Thy will be done; though on earth it be most contrary to ours: Give us this day our daily bread; give us what is meet for us, though it be the bread of tears: Forgive us, especially those sins which we ought to have remembered and did not; as we forgive and pray for those who unknown to us may have transgressed against us: Lead us not into temptation; rather deny, if need be, the thing that we most desire: but deliver us from evil, especially from that evil, which we may be ignorantly wishing and praying for.'

Thus having called on our Lord in His own prayer, and tried to do so, as near as might be, in His own mind, we go on to the special point whatever it be which especially troubles ourselves or the whole Church at the particular time when we offer the Litany: for the collects and short verses and answers which follow do undoubtedly suppose that we are in a time of trouble, though the words spoken do not express any particular kind of trouble. But first we prepare ourselves for such earnest application to our Lord by acknowledging ourselves unworthy in a strain from the holy Psalmist: 'O Lord, deal not with us after our sins. Neither reward us according to our iniquities.' As much as to say that we know we have deserved both to be rejected while we pray, and to find no fruit of our prayers afterwards: but we trust in that mercy which taught God's ancient people, however backsliding, to say and sing in their psalms, 'Thou hast not dealt with us after our sins, nor rewarded us according to our wickednesses; for our sins have reached up to heaven, but Thou, by our gracious Redeemer, hast set them as far from us as heaven from earth: and our wickednesses are a sore burden, but Thou hast taken on Thee both them and the far greater burden of Thine own Cross:' and so we, even such as we, are bold to say to one another, 'Let us pray:' and to plead with our Lord in that affecting prayer, which begins, 'O God, merciful Father.' Observe, brethren, the course of that prayer. The address, or usual acknowledgment rendered to God at the beginning, is, 'O God, merciful Father,

Who despisest not the sighing of the contrite heart, nor the desire of such as be sorrowful:' as much as to say, 'We venture to come before Thee, knowing that Thou never scornest those in distress, and we are sure that we are in distress: and knowing also that Thou never turnest a deaf ear to the lowest sigh which can be breathed from a contrite heart, and though we dare not call ourselves contrite, yet we hope that we are trying to be so:' and in that hope we proceed to offer up to Him two petitions: first, that He would be with us in our prayers in the present trouble, whatever it be: 'Mercifully assist our prayers that we make before Thee in all our troubles and adversities, whensoever they oppress us;' as much as to say, 'We do not ask to be free from troubles and adversities; we know what we deserve, and what we must expect: we do not even ask that those troubles may never oppress us; that our hearts may never sink under them; that they may never seem like a sore burden, too heavy for us to bear: to all this we make up our minds, for all this Thy saints have borne, and do bear, and what are we, that we should think to be better off than they? but what we do humbly and earnestly ask is, that Thou wouldest be with us in such sore troubles and trials, both inward and outward, to teach us how to pray, and to help us while we are praying.'

On the Litany. VIII.

So much we ask, in respect of all evils in general: and then we go on to speak of one class of evils in particular; those evils, namely, which the craft and subtlety of the devil or man worketh against us. You see by the Church's instructing us so to pray that she takes it as a thing not to be doubted, that we as Christians must expect to have evil at all times being wrought against us, not only by the devil, but also by man, and that in a crafty and subtle way. Not of course that each one of us without exception has personal enemies, fellow-creatures who hate him and are plotting to do him mischief: for I trust that *that* is a rare thing, although in our complaining and ill-tempered ways we are apt not seldom to imagine it: but as we all have one crafty and subtle enemy, the devil, who is never tired of contriving how to ruin us, so a great portion of the world being blinded by him, and led captive at his will, is really engaged in harming us by subtle ways, even though it bear no particular malice against us: e. g. people who do not like strictness and self-denial will always be sharp and subtle in devising ways to put those out of countenance who in earnest try to follow Christ as well as they can. They will scorn and tease a man for being exact and particular in his duties: and this in a small way is an instance of the warfare which is always going on, on a large scale, between the world and the Church: everywhere and in all times there will always be two kingdoms and two parties, the Church and the world, believers and unbelievers; and as it was in S. Paul's time, even so it is now: 'he that is born after the flesh' will manage, craftily if he, cannot openly, to 'persecute him who is born after the Spirit.' This is the condition which the Litany supposes us to be in. Persecution, crafty and subtle, our state; contrition and godly sorrow, our mind; and thankfulness to God in His holy Church, our end. For thus we go on to pray, 'graciously hear us that those evils, which the craft and subtlety of the devil or man worketh against us, be brought to nought, and by the providence of Thy goodness they may be dispersed:' i.e. that in Thine own good time Thou wouldest scatter and frustrate whatever the world or the devil in their deepest and most cunning ways may contrive against us: as it is in the Psalm, '*a* Let God arise, and let His enemies be scattered. Like as the smoke vanisheth, so shalt Thou drive them away; and like as wax melteth at the fire, so let the ungodly perish at the Presence of God. But let the righteous be glad and rejoice before God; let them also be merry and joyful:' which at latest will be in the hour of our death, if we are faithful: and therefore those verses

* Ps. lxviii. 1-3.

are often used in the Church by the deathbed of a penitent Christian. But in the meantime we have need of patience: we must not expect our deliverance all at once: as the Church signifies where she says, 'By the providence of Thy goodness, they may be dispersed:' for providence looks far onwards, and when we here speak of it, we naturally think of tarrying and waiting patiently. In the meantime our request is, not that there may be no persecutions, but that we may be such true servants of God, that no persecutions may hurt us: i.e. that none may hurt us indeed, or for ever: that none may hurt our souls, nor turn us out of the Church, nor hinder us from giving thanks to God evermore as part of that holy and happy company: 'That we Thy servants, being hurt by no persecutions, may evermore give thanks unto Thee in Thy holy Church.'

This is the prayer, and, instead of the usual Amen, the Church directs the congregation to answer, 'O Lord, arise, help us, and deliver us for Thy Name's sake.' This circumstance, being so unusual, marks the depth of the Church's distress: she takes up a word from holy David, and Daniel, and from the other Prophets, for they often plead with God by His great Name: taking the hint as it seems from Moses, who, making intercession for Israel, saith, '[b] What

[b] Josh. vii. 9.

wilt Thou do unto Thy great Name?' so here we cry out with one voice, 'O Lord, arise, help us, and deliver us for Thy Name's sake.' God's Name may be pleaded in behalf of Christians even more than in behalf of Israel, for never were the Israelites made partakers of His Name in the mysterious way in which we Christians are in the Sacrament of Holy Baptism, when we are made one with Him, 'c partakers of the Divine Nature.' And when we say 'for Thy Name's sake,' we put Him in mind both of what He is in Himself, and of what He has made Himself, if so be He will be merciful. Then the priest, following as it were the note which the congregation has sounded for him, utters a voice from the book of Psalms, 'd O God, we have heard with our ears, and our fathers have declared unto us, the noble works that Thou didst in their days, and in the old time before them.' It is the first verse of that Psalm which more exactly perhaps than any other seems as we read or hear it to prophesy the present broken and decayed state of God's Church: and very comfortable it is to be allowed, as our fathers were, to put God in mind of His noble deeds and miracles of mercy wrought of old time and declared unto us by our fathers, both in their days and in the ages long before them: one generation handing on to another

^c 2 S. Pet. i. 4.   ^d Ps. xliv. 1.

the lamp of Truth and the watchword of Hope. And then once more the congregation pleads with Him by His own honour and glory; 'O Lord, arise, help us, and deliver us for Thine honour:' as though we should say, 'Deliver us, for else the enemy will say, He could not, or would not be their God, and so I have prevailed against them.' After which both priest and people join in the hymn of glory, praising Him devoutly in the midst of their cries or distress, saying the Gloria Patri on their knees, like holy Job when he cried out, 'Though He slay me, yet will I put my trust in Him.'

So be it, O Lord, with us always, in all our afflictions, in all that we have to bear, whether each one for himself, or together as members of Thy Church. As the clouds gather, as the distress increases, may we still more earnestly give Thee glory, humbling ourselves under Thy mighty hand, and casting all our care upon Thee; and we shall soon find how truly Thou carest for us.

SERMON IX.

ON THE LITANY. IX.

CONCLUSION.

PSALM xxxiii. 22.

Let Thy merciful kindness, O Lord, be upon us, like as we do put our trust in Thee.

WE left off last week at that part of the Litany, where, in the very midst of her deepest complaint and misery, the Holy Church breaks out into a hymn of glory to God: saying the Gloria Patri on her knees. In the midst, I say, of her complaint and misery: for just before she had been pleading with her God and Lord by the remembrance of His noble works of old time: 'Arise, and help us, and deliver us for Thy Name's sake; Arise, and help us, and deliver us for Thine honour.' Then comes the Gloria Patri, and immediately after it, all is again in the tone of sadness and alarm: 'From our enemies defend us, O Christ; graciously look upon our afflictions.' Do you not see how exactly it answers to the faithful and loving words of the most patient of men, holy Job: how even in darkness and the shadow of death, when all seemed not only most painful, but also hardest and most unaccountable, even then he holds fast by the Saviour Who seemed to have deserted him? As that poor woman came behind our Lord, and touched the hem of His garment, not counting herself worthy to see His face: as the other, the blessed woman of Canaan still continued calling upon Him, though He turned away and hid His face from her, yea, even though He made as if He was scorning her; so the holy Job, true type of the Man of sorrows, had made up his mind never to cease trusting in God: though his misery go on from want to desolation, and from desolation to sickness, and from sickness to reproach, and from reproach to persecution, and from persecution to death, he will not cease trusting in the Lord[a]: he will adore the hand that lays the stripes upon him. Is not this just like the holy Church our mother in this part of the Litany? It is not that she does not feel her distress, and feel it too very bitterly; she knows what it is to be persecuted and oppressed, to have 'the craft and subtlety of the devil and man' working against her; she is not dead and insensible to all this; rather the iron enters into her very soul, and she pleads most earnestly with her God and Father, by all His past mercies, to

[a] Job xiii. 15.

deliver her. But in all her complaint, in all her earnest supplication, she is childlike and confiding, she clings to Him Who is chastening her, and therefore (for I will repeat it once more, wishing that we all take notice of it) she gives glory to the Lord on her knees; or rather when she is lying prostrate before Him, humbled to the dust by her sins and the sins of her forefathers. Though He slay her, yet will she put her trust in Him: nevertheless, she still feels that He is slaying her, and renews accordingly her loud and bitter cry, in the short verses and answers which immediately follow. In the first of these we make mention of our enemies, in the second of our afflictions, in the third of our sorrows, and in the fourth of our sins. 'From our enemies defend us, O Christ,' i. e. especially, the enemies of our souls, the evil spirits and evil men, who sometimes knowing what they do, sometimes from ignorance, and not caring what comes of their conduct, are but too busy in helping us along the broad way. Then we put Him in mind of our afflictions: we plead with Him, as persons asking charity commonly plead, by simply telling Him how very miserable we are; how very much we long to have but a look from Him: we urge Him to look upon us as the Psalmist said: pleading not any good thing in ourselves, but only our great load of troubles: 'graciously look upon our afflictions.' In this, as almost always, we follow the

On the Litany. IX.

Psalmist's pattern: '^b Look upon my adversity, and forgive me all my sin.'

Next, from outward afflictions we go on to inward sorrows: for such I take to be the difference of the two clauses, 'Graciously look upon our afflictions,' and 'Pitifully behold the sorrows of our hearts.' We pray our only and most loving Father, the Creator of our souls and minds and hearts as well as of our bodies, not only to spare these our weak and frail bodies, but to have compassion also on the wayward and infirm, the fallen and sinful spirits, which dwell in these bodies, and suffer so grievously with them: which also have so many trials and passions of their own, so many fears, griefs, regrets, suspicions, jealousies, discontents: arising indeed often from mere fancy, mere dreams of disordered imagination, but in the misery they cause not at all unreal nor fanciful: the deepest of sorrows to those who feel them, though in themselves the merest dreams. Concerning all these, as well as all afflictions from without, the Church here instructs us to pray that our Lord would pitifully behold them, and we cannot have the smallest doubt that He will do so, since He hath Himself taught us by His Holy Spirit that He can be touched with a feeling of all our innocent infirmities. Nay more, my brethren, we are permitted in a way to plead our very sins before God as

^b Ps. xxv. 17.

a kind of reason why He should forgive us: for our sins that are past do beyond all things show how very helpless we are, since of ourselves we cannot clear our consciences of any part of any one of them : there are the stains, there is the guilt, and there it must abide for ever, if He take not pity upon us. Therefore, as I said, our very sins may be mentioned in our prayers as a reason why He should pity us : as we find over and over in the Psalms: 'c Innumerable troubles are come about me; my sins have taken such hold upon me that I am not able to look up: yea, they are more in number than the hairs of my head, and my heart hath failed me.' What follows? Am I therefore to leave off prayer? Is there no hope? Is all lost? Nay, in the very next verse we read, 'O Lord, let it be Thy pleasure to deliver me; make haste, O Lord, to help me.' So in these earnest breathings, these quick dartings of prayer, which we find in this portion of the Litany : having mentioned our enemies, our afflictions and sorrows, we go on to mention our sins : ' Mercifully forgive the sins of Thy people :' of Thy people, brethren, observe *that:* for it makes a very great difference. The sins of God's people are as much worse than the same sins in others who are not God's people, as their helps and privileges and graces are greater, as the Truth itself hath told us : 'd Unto whom men have

c Ps. xl. 15.   d S. Luke xii. 48.

On the Litany. IX.

committed much, of him they will ask the more.' Therefore it is a great thing indeed, for the people of God to ask for *their* sins to be forgiven, and we could hardly have ventured to do so, had He not so mercifully encouraged us. I wish we thought more of this than we are apt to do. We have heard so much of His pardoning love from our very cradles upward, that there is too much fear of our saying this petition and others like it with a sort of unconcern, as if what we were asking for was an ordinary thing, a matter of course. O let us endeavour to cure ourselves of this, for indeed it is a great and a very dangerous mistake! Our wilful sins, inasmuch as they are the sins of God's people, cannot be ordinary things, matters of course, nor is it an ordinary mercy for Him to forgive them, but a very miracle of grace. Unless we pray very earnestly to have them forgiven, pray with somewhat of a true feeling what a great thing we are praying for, we shall not feel half the fear which we ought of falling into the same sins or worse again. The tempter will have a great advantage over us.

And there is another thought, which may sometimes well come into a Christian's mind, when he prays this short prayer, 'Mercifully forgive the sins of Thy people.' It is this: that not only particular persons, men and women, are continually sinning and needing forgiveness, but the whole Church also and the people of God, and much more a particular portion of it, such as the Church of England or the Church of Rome, may fall into sin, and bring God's anger upon it: as we read in Solomon's prayer at the Dedication of the temple, all the way through mention is made of the sins of God's people Israel, and God is asked to forgive them, as well as to forgive the several sins of the men and women of whom that people is made up. Now, without undutifully judging of our mother the Church: since it is made of men, and there is no man that sinneth not, we may well believe that the Church also has its sins, for which we may and ought to pray to God to forgive it: and it is well that this should sometimes come into our mind, when we beseech Him to forgive the sins of His people. As a man's parents may and do sin, without ceasing to be his parents, so the Church to which he belongs, or the whole Church of his time, may sin, without ceasing to be a Church: and as it is his duty to ask forgiveness for his parents' sins, so also for the Church's sins, whether he knows of any special sin or not. Who can doubt that the Laodicean Christians in S. John's time were bound to pray that God would mercifully forgive the sin of lukewarmness, which Christ Himself declared to be their Church's sin, saying, 'e Because thou art lukewarm, and neither cold nor hot, I will spue thee out of My

* Rev. iii. 16.

mouth?' It is not impossible, surely, that the Church of England in our time, or any particular portion of it, may be in the same sin, and in danger of the same dreadful sentence. O then how earnestly ought we to pray that He would pardon and amend this great sin of lukewarmness, not in ourselves only, but in our whole Church and nation! that in His tender love He would rebuke and chasten us, if so be we would be zealous and repent!

Having thus mentioned before God our enemies, our afflictions, our sorrows, and our sins, we dart another short petition upwards, like a sort of Amen, to confirm and recommend all our other petitions: 'Favourably with mercy hear our prayers;' favourably, for we know too well how much favour they need, how poor and unworthy they are in themselves: with mercy, forgiving the many sins and negligences of which, even in these very prayers, since we knelt down, we know ourselves to be guilty.

And this great indulgence we are the more hopeful to ask, because, as the next short petition expresses, He permits us to call Him Son of David: 'O Son of David, have mercy upon us:' words taken, as you know, from the lips of the blind men who sat by the wayside as our Lord was journeying near Jericho: and well used by us sinners in our Litany, because of David's being both a great king over God's people, and in one instance a great sinner; and the Litany, as we have seen, is especially put up for God's people, and most especially asks to have their sins forgiven and cured. By allowing us thus to call Him Son of David, He gives us a token that He never can forget His Church, nor ever fail in most tender mercy towards any returning penitent.

Then we acknowledge to Him that we need His mercy not now only, but at all times; we take Him to be our God for ever and ever: for such is the meaning of the next short prayer, 'Both now and ever, vouchsafe to hear us, O Christ.' As much as to say, '[f] Whom have we in heaven but Thee? and there is none upon earth that we desire in comparison of Thee. My flesh and my heart faileth, but God is the strength of my heart, and my portion for ever.' Well will it be with us when we can pray this prayer in earnest.

Once again we call Him Christ and our Lord Christ, and beseech Him graciously to hear us: like eager petitioners who will not be put off, 'Graciously hear us, O Christ; graciously hear us, O Lord Christ.' And then, before passing into the form of collect again, as we do in the end of the Litany, we profess to Him, in a few of His own perfect words, both what we desire of Him, and in what mind we express our desire. 'Let Thy merciful kindness, O Lord, be upon us: like as

[f] Ps. lxxiii. 25, 26.

we do put our trust in Thee.' That is the verse which the Church has taken from the end of the thirty-third Psalm, and transplanted it, as it were, to be the last of her short petitions in the Litany: whereby she teaches us out of the mouth of God this very serious truth, that free as His mercy is, it yet in some mysterious way is made to depend on our trust in Him: so that we may only venture to ask for it in proportion as we trust in Him: even as in the Lord's Prayer we are instructed by Himself to ask for our own pardon only in such measure as we are willing to pardon others. Thus our Father would bind us to our duty by our prayers. We seek for so much mercy from our Lord, as we bring to our prayers of dutiful trust in Him. Alas, for the repining, dissatisfied spirits, who come to their prayers with downcast, dismal hearts, because their worldly affairs do not go on exactly to their wish! and alas (no less), for the prosperous and thriving, if they allow their prosperity and hopefulness to carry them away from Him Who is their only sure hope! if, while they say with their lips these lowly words of the Church, they are in their hearts depending on their own skill, their own wealth or good luck! Sad or joyous, they are alike wrong, because their hearts are alike set upon this world.

You know how in the Collect which follows, the substance of the whole Litany is gathered, after the manner of collects, into a few words. 'We humbly beseech Thee, O Father, mercifully to look upon our infirmities; and for the glory of Thy Name turn from us all those evils that we most righteously have deserved.' See what real lowliness we are practising, when we try to enter into the mind of such a prayer as this: how deeply sensible we must be, not of infirmities only but of ill-deserts, and observe what follows; 'For the glory of Thy Name turn from us all those evils that we most righteously have deserved; and grant, that in all our troubles we may put our whole trust and confidence in Thy mercy, and evermore serve Thee in holiness and pureness of living, to Thy honour and glory.' We do not pray for deliverance so much, as for perfect trust in Him, and for a holy and pure life. Troubles and adversities, we take for granted, must be our portion, only we beseech Him that they may not separate us from Him, nor take away our power of serving Him: but whether that service shall be in doing or in suffering we leave to Him.

After this, as you know, come in the occasional collects: for the parliament, the Ember weeks, and others. These I will not now notice: but there is one prayer which always comes in here, the General Thanksgiving, added to our Litany after the Church's sufferings in the time of the great rebellion, and written by a holy Bishop, who had been a sufferer in those bad times, Bishop Sanderson. You who come here constantly know this thanksgiving well: will you try and remember one or two things, quite necessary to the right use of it? The first, that as it is a *general* thanksgiving, for all our brethren as well as for ourselves, no envious, grudging heart ought to dare to use it. The second, that whereas we often mention the names of persons for whom we offer thanks, there is need of care, as there is when we pray for persons by name: that we really care for those persons, that we really join with the Church in what she says of them: that they should not be to us names merely said over by rote. Thirdly, you know that in this thanksgiving we profess to be grateful 'above all for the redemption of the world by our Lord Jesus Christ, for the means of grace, and for the hope of glory.' Evidently we cannot say this truly, unless we are really trying to care more for heaven than for anything else: there must be the right hope, the hope of glory: the right means, the means of grace, that is, the holy Sacraments with all helps to the due receiving of them, and the right foundation for both, i.e. the God-Man offering Himself on the Cross. See how much this one portion of the holy service requires of us: and besides, if we have joined in it truly, we of course go out of Church as persons going from a solemn sacrifice of thanksgiving: still as we go, and whatever we go to, offering up ourselves, our souls and bodies, to serve Him thankfully in holiness and righteousness.

Then comes the prayer of the holy father, S. Chrysostom: where we plead our Lord's ancient promise to two or three gathered in His Name, and His present providential mercy to us in allowing us to be so gathered: and see what entire trust and childlike faith the Church supposes in us, putting this prayer into our mouths: for in it we absolutely leave all other things to God; only two things there are, which He has promised, and which He encourages us to claim: and we may claim them the more hopefully, the more entirely we trust Him with everything else that we care for: knowledge of His truth here, and life everlasting in the world to come.

And so the Church dismisses us with the benediction of S. Paul, 'The grace of our Lord Jesus Christ, and the love of God, and the fellowship of the Holy Ghost, be with us all evermore,' which is specially suited to the Litany, because it mentions the grace of our Lord *first:* the two other portions of the blessing, the love of the Father, and the Communion of the Spirit, being purchased entirely for us by Christ. Now this is just the order of the Litany: in which, as you heard, the special petitions are all made to Christ the great Intercessor, to be by Him presented to the Father, and made fruitful to us through the Spirit.

So you see our Litany at its end gathers in one three voices, of very holy persons, Bishop Sanderson, S. Chrysostom, and S. Paul: a beautiful example of the Communion of Saints. May God in His mercy cause us to pray with them now, that with them we may thank Him for ever! And may He ever bless our use of the Litany, and make it a real help to us in these sorrowful times!

Amen
Lord Jesus

SERMON X[a].

THE CHURCH ONE.

1 S. JOHN v. 8.

There are three that bear witness in earth, the Spirit, and the water, and the Blood; and these three agree in one.

OUR Saviour Himself has in some sort appointed for us a subject, on which we should meditate during this holy season; this joyful season, between Easter and Whitsuntide. He Himself prepared His disciples for the Descent of the Holy Ghost by speaking to them of the things pertaining to the kingdom of God. Our Lord was that noble Person of Whom He Himself had spoken a little before in parable [b], Who was departing to receive to Himself a kingdom and return. And His discoursing with His Apostles on the things of His kingdom, what was it, but that same nobleman calling unto Him His servants, and delivering unto them His goods, and bidding them, 'Occupy till I come?'

[a] *Marked* Catech. on the Church 1.
[b] S. Luke xix. 11-13.

But what is this kingdom of God, which we are to think so much of at all times, and especially now? In a word, it is the Church of Christ, that society, company, or brotherhood, into which it is His purpose to gather us all, that we may be happy with Him for ever. It is called His kingdom, just as we say the kingdom of France or of England; just as the twelve tribes of Israel were called the kingdom of David. The kingdom of Christ means all the persons who are subject to Jesus Christ: who are bound to obey Him, not only as He is God over all, blessed for ever, but also as He is in particular their own proper King and Head. The kingdom of Christ, I say, means *all* who are thus subject to Christ, at all times: both those who are now on their training in this imperfect world, and those who now or hereafter shall be taken up and made perfect in Paradise and in Heaven. Just as the little child in his weakness is nevertheless the same person as the full-grown man in his strength, so the Church militant on earth, with its sins and imperfections, is nevertheless the same kingdom with the Church made perfect and triumphant in Heaven.

Our Lord, during the whole time of His abode among us in the flesh, was preparing for this kingdom; preparing and training up His Apostles to be governors in it, and all around Him to acknowledge and obey it, when it should be set up in their sight.

But it was not set up, until He was gone up to His Father's Right Hand. On Ascension Day He, as our King, sate down on His Throne on high: and ten days afterwards He sent His Spirit, as you know, on Whitsunday, to declare and establish His holy kingdom, by winning and gathering into it, one by one, the souls of His redeemed. So that we are able to point out exactly the day and hour when the kingdom of heaven began: not only the very day, but the very hour. The day, I need not tell you, was the Day of Pentecost, fifty days after our Lord's Resurrection. It was the first Whitsunday, fifty days after the first Easter Day. And the hour was the third hour, i.e. nine o'clock in the morning: so S. Peter tells us, in his sermon which he made just after the Holy Ghost had come down. On their all speaking with tongues, some of the profane multitudes said, it was only that they were full of new wine. But the Apostle replies, 'ᶜThese are not drunken, as ye suppose, seeing it is but the third hour of the day,' not later than nine in the morning. So exactly has the Holy Spirit informed us of the very time of His descent; we know, to an hour, how long it is since our Lord's kingdom was set up. And we can trace it all along in history, even from that time to this. The grain of mustard-seed then sown has grown into a great tree; the leaven has

ᶜ Acts ii. 15.

spread through the whole three measures of meal; the vine brought out of Egypt has had room made for it, it hath waxen great, and filled the earth.

But the great point for each one of us to consider and lay to heart is, that we ourselves are members of this body, sheep of this fold, branches of this tree, citizens of this kingdom. Our hope of eternal life depends upon this. For as we are born in sin, so in sin we must die, unless we have been new-born in Christ, made members of His Body. And if by any fault of ours we cut ourselves off from the Church, we cut ourselves off from Christ. Therefore we have been taught from the beginning to think very much of the Holy Catholic Church: we pray in the Lord's Prayer that it may come more and more perfectly; in the Creed we profess to believe it: every year we keep the holy Feast of Whitsuntide; we keep it with especial devotion, because it is the Birthday of the Church.

And the same Creeds which teach us that there is a Church, instruct us also in certain things, pertaining to the Church, which it highly concerns us to know. For if we are not in the Church, we are not in the kingdom of God, nor in the way to heaven: even as no one was in the way to be saved from perishing by the waters of the flood, save those who were in the ark. Therefore it is well for us to know what marks and tokens it has pleased God to set upon the true Church; that we may be the more thankful for our own happiness in having been made members of it, and the more careful never to wander from it, either by unbelief or wilful separation, or by any other sin.

Now the first thing plainly taught us in the Creeds concerning the Church is this—that it is One. There is but one true Church; there cannot be more. We speak indeed of many Churches, the Church of England, the Church of France, the Church of Russia, the Church of Canada, and so on; just as S. Paul speaks of the several Churches of Galatia: but still these are but parts or members of the one Holy Church throughout the world: much in the same way as England and Scotland and Ireland are parts and members of one United Kingdom. This, both our Creeds declare. The Nicene Creed, which we use at every Communion, uses the very word One: 'I believe One Catholic and Apostolic Church:' one only, and no more. The Apostles' Creed, our baptismal Creed, the Creed which I trust we are accustomed to say daily with our prayers, does not indeed expressly call the Church *one*; but it plainly signifies that the Church is but one, in that it instructs us to say, 'I believe in *the* Holy Catholic Church.' When people speak in that way, it always means that the thing so spoken of is single; that there is no other besides it: as when a child says, I must honour and obey *the* Queen, one knows that it means our own Queen and no other; and when Scripture mentions '*the* holy city,' we understand it to mean Jerusalem, and no other place: so to believe in *the* Church must mean believing that there is one society, one company, one brotherhood, one kingdom of heaven, to which all who are to be saved must belong.

And what the Creeds thus teach in short, Holy Scripture affirms and teaches at large, in a great many ways, and by a great variety of parables: and, (but chiefly and above all,) we may understand that the Church must be one and one only, by considering that it is the Body of Christ. Christ is One, and His Body is One, and the Church is His Body, therefore the Church must needs be One. As surely as there is but one Christ, so surely is there but one Church. S. Paul puts it in as plain words as possible, '[d] As the body is one, and hath many members, and all the members of that one body, being many, are one body, so also is Christ. For by one Spirit we are all baptized into one body, whether we be Jews or Gentiles, whether we be bond or free.' So it is: the meanest beggar, who has been baptized into Christ, is as truly a member of Christ as the greatest king: and what is still more

[d] 1 Cor. xii. 12, 13.

aweful and astonishing, the mere ordinary Christian, until his sins have become so bad as to cut him off from the body, is as truly and really in Christ (though much more unworthily), as S. Paul or S. Peter was. It is a strange and fearful thought, but so it is.

For as the whole race of mankind are naturally one by their common head and root, Adam, so the whole race of Christians, the holy seed, the Lord's nation and family, are one, in a way beyond nature, by their adoption or engrafting into one spiritual Root and Head, Jesus Christ. In Him, we all of us are by grace, as we are in the first Adam by our first conception and birth. The whole Church is in a manner formed and taken out of Him, as Eve, the first woman, was formed and taken out of Adam. Eve, being naturally the mother of us all, is the type and figure of the Church, our spiritual mother. The creation of Eve answers in a wonderful manner to the building up of the Church. For thus it stands in Holy Scripture. First, the Lord, having determined to make an help-meet for Adam, caused a deep sleep to fall upon him, and he slept. So when the Father would form and build up that Church which was ordained from all eternity to be the Mystical Body of His Son, He caused the deep sleep of death, even the death of the Cross, to fall upon Him, Who is our second Adam. He sleeps, the Son of God sleeps in death, hanging on the Cross; and while He is asleep, the Lord permits His side to be pierced. Adam's side, as you know, was pierced by the Hand of the Almighty Himself: but This Man's Side by one of the heathen soldiers, who, finding Him dead when he did not expect to do so, ran his spear into His Side (His Right Side, so it is commonly believed) and forthwith came there out blood and water.

Well, so far is plain enough, that there is a sort of likeness between the way in which our Lord's Side was pierced, after He was dead on the Cross, and the way in which Adam's side had been pierced, so many ages before, in his deep and death-like slumber. But that which ensued when our Lord's Side was pierced— what, one may ask, has it to do with the formation and building up, either of the Church, or of Eve who is the type of the Church? How does the one at all answer to the other? Very well indeed, my brethren, if you will consider the matter with earnestness and reverence. Imagine, first, the Lord God, how having opened Adam's side He took out one of the ribs, and the rib which He had taken out of the man He builded up, formed by degrees, into a woman. Then consider what it was that flowed out of our Lord's Side when it had been pierced as He hung on the Cross. It was water and blood: and that there was in it some very deep and mysterious meaning, we are sure by

S. John's way of speaking of it, both in his Gospel and in his Epistle. In his Gospel, after relating it, as if it were a very remarkable thing indeed, he adds, '[e] And he that saw it bare record, and his record is true: and he knoweth that he saith true, that ye might believe.' In his Epistle, '[f] This is He that came by Water and Blood, even Jesus Christ; and it is the Spirit that beareth witness, because the Spirit is Truth,' and a little after, 'For there are three that bear witness in earth, the Spirit and the Water and the Blood, and these three agree in one. If we receive the witness of men, the witness of God is greater: for this is the witness of God, which He hath testified of His Son.' As if he should say, Do you not know what the Lord's tokens are, by which we are assured of the Presence of His Son among us according to His promise, 'I am with you always, even unto the end of the world?' Yes, surely: we all know that His abiding tokens are His Sacraments. Pardon and grace, both in Baptism and in Holy Communion, the pardon bought and figured by Blood, the grace represented and conveyed by water: and as the two, pardon and grace, go together in Christ's Sacraments, which have all their virtue from His death, so the two, Blood and Water, issued out of His pierced Side, but not until

[e] S. John xix. 35.   [f] 1 S. John v. 6.

after that He had given up the ghost. And now comes the point which answers to the formation of the first woman: as she was gradually builded up out of that which was taken from Adam's side, so is the Church builded up out of that which came from our Lord's Side. For what is the building up of the Church, but the gradual addition to it of fresh members, living stones, as it were, by the Sacrament of Baptism, and the gradual growth and advancement of those, who are already members, by the Sacrament of the Holy Eucharist? And the Church is thus builded up to be our Lord's Spouse: as Eve, when God had finished building her up, was brought unto Adam, and became his wife; and he acknowledged her to be bone of his bone and flesh of his flesh, in words which were afterwards taken up by the Holy Spirit to declare Christ's union with His Mystical Body the Church and with every living member of it. '[g] The Lord loveth and cherisheth the Church : for we are members of His Body, *of* His Flesh and *of* His Bones : for this cause shall a man leave his father and mother and shall be joined unto his wife, and they two shall be one flesh. This is a great mystery: I mean, as to Christ and the Church.' The Church then is builded up to be a Spouse; not many spouses, but one: the

[g] Eph. v. 29-32.

Bride, the Lamb's wife, she of whom it had been written, 'ʰ My Dove, my undefiled, is one.' And as at the beginning there was no divorce, nor any multiplying of wives, so was it never heard or read of that Christ should have more than one Spouse, the true, ancient, Catholic and Apostolic Church.

And as the Church is in itself the One mystical Body of Christ, so the manner of its building up is such as to show very remarkably how earnestly our Lord's heart longs to behold us all *one*. Each living stone, each new member in the Body, is added on gradually by the Spirit blessing the Water and the Blood, i.e. by the pardon conveyed and grace bestowed through the Spirit in the Sacraments. It seems to the eye as if there were many priests, many baptizers, going on continually with this work. But faith knows and remembers that as there is but one Baptism and one Holy Eucharist, so there is among us but one Priest, properly so called; and one Baptizer, viz. the Lord Jesus Christ, Who alone baptizeth with the Holy Ghost. As it is one Body, the Body of Christ; one Spirit, the Spirit of Christ; so is it one Lord and King, one Faith and form of sound words, one Baptism and one Eucharist. Outwardly indeed there appear to be very many, and men are apt to fancy that the blessing depends more or less on the minister: but it is not

ʰ Cant. vi. 9.

so, for the true Minister always and in every place is Christ.

You see then in part, brethren, the Unity of the Church, what it is. The whole Church is our Lord's *one* Body; the Spirit of Christ blessing His Sacraments is the *one* mean of union with that Body; Christ Himself is the *one* true Priest and baptizer. So entirely is the Catholic and Apostolical Church *one*: and that by virtue of our Lord's Intercession: '[1] I pray, not for My disciples only, but for those whom Thou hast given Me by their word: that they may all be One.'

Christ calls us to be one in Him: for this He prayed; for this He shed out of His most precious Side both water and blood. He would have His Church all one: one outwardly by loving communion in holy services, especially in His Sacraments; as it cannot but be one inwardly by the spiritual union of each of its members to Him. See then, what sin a person commits, who wilfully damages this unity. He contradicts his Lord's dying prayer: he makes void, so far, the purpose for which He poured out His Blood on the Cross. Little do they think of this, who go so freely to all sorts of places to worship; a thing too common in our times; not caring whether it is the Church, in communion with which they so worship, or

[1] S. John xvii. 20, 21.

some of the many dissenters from the Church. They mean, sometimes, not amiss; they go to hear that which is good: but indeed they know not what they do. We on the other hand, who have learned from the Scripture that there is but one Church, but one Body of Christ; we, if we separate from that Body or do anything that tends towards separation, can hardly say that we know not what we do. We must bear our burden as wilful disturbers of Christ's Peace; wilfully breaking ourselves off from the true Vine; and how then can we any more bear good fruit?

And remember, my brethren, that it is separating one's self, not only when people go to some other sort of worship, but when they allow themselves to go nowhere at all. It is schism, i. e. division, to stay away from the Holy Communion, as well as to seek for it in places apart from Christ's Church. Remember these things now, that you may not be tempted to break the bonds of unity, by going another way, for diversion's sake or company's sake, when you ought to be going to Church. And again, remember these things bye and bye; for you may be tried in other ways: you may change your abode, or go to service, and be thrown among people who know not what the Church is, and who imagine that it does not much signify where one worships. Then say in your heart, 'my dying Saviour prayed that His Church might be

One; He poured out blood and water from His Heart for a token of those Sacraments which were to make and keep it one. God forbid that we should separate ourselves from it, or do any thing at all to divide it!' God give us grace to make more and more of His Sacraments: which alone, worthily received, by virtue of the Spirit which is in them will make and keep us one in Him.

SERMON XI[a].

THE CHURCH CATHOLIC.

1 TIM. ii. 4.

Who will have all men to be saved, and to come to the knowledge of the Truth.

As the Church or Body of Christ, the Kingdom of God, is One, and One only, so also it is *Catholic:* and this is the second point which we learn in the Creed concerning it: 'I believe One Catholic and Apostolic Church:' or as it stands in the Apostles' Creed, 'I believe in the Holy Catholic Church.' How it is One, even a child may perceive, by such parables and sayings of Christ and the Apostles, as I put you in mind of last Sunday. To-day you have heard something about what is meant when we call the Church, *Catholic:* and it is a point which it nearly concerns us all, especially in these days, to consider and recollect.

Now Catholic, as many of you know, is just a Greek word signifying Universal. The holy Catho-

[a] *Marked,* 'Catech. on the Church. 2.'

lic Church, in the Apostles' Creed, is just the same with that in the Litany, for which we pray by the name of God's holy Church Universal. And the Church, according to God's gracious will and purpose, was to be Universal, to gather into itself 'all people of all nations and in all generations, unto the end of the world.' It was also to be Universal, by teaching to all its members all necessary and saving truth. The Church is Catholic, because God will have all men to be saved; and the Faith is Catholic, because it is the whole of that Truth, by the knowledge whereof He would have all men to be saved.

At the first indeed, when our Lord was Himself in sight among men, He said, He was sent only to the lost sheep of the house of Israel; and when He sent His disciples on their rounds, He said unto them, '[b]Go not into the way of the Gentiles, and into any city of the Samaritans enter ye not: but go rather unto the lost sheep of the house of Israel.' So it was, until after His Death and Resurrection: it was one of the privileges of the seed of Abraham after the flesh, that they only should be eye-witnesses of the Presence of the Son of God in the flesh. But He had also said (as you heard in the Gospel just now), '[c]Other sheep I have, which are not of this fold: them also I must bring, and they shall

[b] S. Matt. x. 5, 6.   [c] S. John x. 16.

hear My Voice, and there shall be one fold, and one Shepherd;' i.e. Christ had also among the Gentiles those who would believe on Him, when His providence gave them the opportunity to do so. And before long He meant to give them their invitation: the king's servants were to be told to go into the highways and hedges; and from the East and from the West, and from the North and from the South, men were to come and be gathered into the kingdom of God. So He had given notice in very many of His parables; and after His Resurrection, He spake out His meaning more plainly. He met His disciples on the mountain in Galilee, and told them to go and make Christians of all nations. He bade them go into all the world, and preach the Gospel to every creature. So it was before our Saviour departed out of this world. He had declared openly that, at some time or other, the other nations who were not of the seed of Abraham would be admitted into the kingdom of Heaven: but He had not as yet actually sent the message to them. Bye and bye came the great Day of Pentecost; the heavenly kingdom was actually set up, and although the first gathering into it consisted of Israelites only (for it was at Jerusalem among those who had come to keep the feast according to the Law), yet the Holy Ghost, by the mouth of S. Peter, very plainly signified, that it was His Will to give Himself to the other nations also: '^dfor the promise,' He saith, 'is unto you and to your children, and to all that are afar off.' That is, the Holy Church, of which you now see the beginning, is meant by Almighty God to be a Catholic or Universal Church. For what is 'the promise,' of which the Apostle was speaking? The Holy Ghost, Which had been promised to be sent by the Father upon all who should believe and be baptized, to make them members of Christ. That promise, S. Peter says, is unto you; to this present generation of Jews; and not to you only, but to your children; to all generations that shall come after you. That is, the Church was to be universal in point of time; the same body, or family, or kingdom, which began that day at Jerusalem, was to continue until the end of the world, and not even then to come to an end, but to be taken up into heaven, and there made perfect with its Lord for ever. And not only was it for all generations, but for all nations also: as S. Peter goes on and says, 'For all that are afar off;' for those who have hitherto been without the covenant; the Gentiles with the Jews, the uncircumcised with the circumcised. This was S. Peter's declaration on the Day of Pentecost: and it began to be fulfilled when the same S. Peter came to Cor-

---

^d Acts ii. 39.

nelius' house, and the Holy Ghost, after his preaching, came upon Cornelius and the other Gentiles there assembled. Then the promise began to take place on those who were afar off, and it has gone on ever since, and goes on every time that any one is made a member of Christ by Holy Baptism.

So far then is plain, that the Holy Church is Catholic, as being intended for all ages and all nations of men. God meant it to exist everywhere, and at all times. He meant it also for each individual among men, would they receive it. For the Holy Spirit, speaking by S. Paul in the text, says, God our Saviour would have all men to be saved. His redemption is universal: if any lose the benefit of it, the fault lies somewhere else, not in any want of merciful intention on His part. His will and mind is, to be received as a Saviour everywhere, always, and by all. He would have all men everywhere and always 'to come to the knowledge of the Truth.' They are to be saved, not any how, but in coming to the knowledge of the Truth: i.e. to the knowledge of Jesus Christ: for He is '^{e}the Way, the Truth, and the Life:' '^{f}and this is life eternal, to know Thee the only true God, and Jesus Christ Whom Thou hast sent.' We are to know and receive Christ *entirely*, not in part, but wholly, as He

* S. John xiv. 6. ^{f} Ib. xvii. 3.

Is; Perfect God and Perfect Man. In this sense again the Holy Church is Catholic, because it receives and teaches the whole of Christ's truth. Heretics, and those who are out of the Church, may teach, some one portion of it, some another, but the Catholic Church alone teaches the whole Truth, the whole saving doctrine of Christ. Therefore the Spirit Who is the life of the Church is called especially 'the Spirit of Truth,' and our Lord promises, when He shall come, 'g He will guide you into all the Truth.' 'h He shall teach you all things, and bring all things to your remembrance, whatsoever I have said unto you.' The Catholic or Universal Church may be known by its teaching the whole Creed, the whole saving truth of Scripture, to all without distinction of time or place: in England or New Zealand as in Judea; now, as in the days of the Apostles.

Now since it is every Christian's duty, and we have all promised in our Baptism, to believe the articles of the Christian Faith, i. e. the Creed as the Church teaches it out of the Bible, it should seem that in order to know what we are to believe, we have only one thing to do; viz. to take on the Church's authority what the whole Church has always taught as an article of the Christian Faith. We must make out this, according to the best means

g S. John xvi. 13.   h Ib. xiv. 26.

which God has given us *for* making it out: and having found it, we must receive it at once, whether we can understand it, and account for it, or no. E. g. here in England, suppose any one of the simpler sort, any plain unlearned person, wanting to know what is God's Truth, to the knowledge of which he must come in order to be saved. Take any one of ourselves: here we are, in a branch, a portion of Christ's Church: we are not left to find our way each one by himself. By God's special mercy we are in the Church of England, whose rule is, to go by the Scriptures, as they were interpreted always in the Holy Church Universal, before there were in it such breaks and divisions, as now, alas! are too plainly seen. The Church, I say, puts, as it were, the Bible into the hands of each one of us, and says, 'This is the Book of God:' it teaches us also the catechism, especially the Creed, and says, 'This is the meaning of God's Book, for thus it was understood in the Holy ancient Church, when all Christians were evidently one Body.' What can a plain unlearned Christian do better than submit himself to such teaching as that, when God's providence has put him in the way of it? He is not learned himself, to make out the full meaning of God's Word; but here he has a guide on which he can depend, for it walks by the very rule which the Lord ordained; it believes Him speaking plainly in His written Word, and where His Word is not plain, it takes that meaning of it, which has been received by the first Christians and their children, and by all that were afar off, even as many as the Lord our God hath called. For to them, taken altogether, not to any particular sort of them, nor yet to each generation apart, was the promise given, 'I will guide you into all Truth.'

This our Church of England, I say, is especially Catholic in her accounts of the meaning of Scripture, especially to be trusted by her children, because her rule is always to abide by what the whole Church in all times has taught out of Scripture. She holds by S. Paul's sayings; 'ⁱBrethren, stand fast, and hold the traditions which ye have been taught:' and again, 'ᵏThough we, or an Angel from heaven, preach any other Gospel unto you, than that which we have preached unto you, let him be accursed.' But the other Christian bodies around us, who would tempt us away from the Church of England, do not hold by these sayings of S. Paul. The one sort says, 'Care not for past times, nor Creeds, nor ordained teachers: read or hear your Bible for yourself, and whatsoever you honestly think you find there, that is the Gospel for you.' Go where you will, you will meet, I fear, with too many of this way of thinking:

ⁱ 2 Thess. ii. 15.   ᵏ Gal. i. 8.

and you will sometimes perhaps meet with another sort, with those, I mean, of the Church of Rome, who will likewise say to you, 'Trouble not yourself about times past: do not enquire whether what you are taught is the word which was heard in the Church from the beginning: the only thing you need ask is, whether it is taught by the Bishop of Rome, whom men call the Pope, now.' Both ways, you see, the rule is different from that which is laid down in the Bible. For whether a man goes by his own understanding only, or by the judgement of the Bishop of Rome only, either way he gives up the notion of holding by the old traditions, the Gospel which S. Paul preached, the word which was heard from the beginning, the doctrine received 'everywhere, always, and by all.' Either way he declines submitting himself to the whole Church, which yet is said in Scripture to be the 'pillar and ground of the truth.' But the Church of England teaches us to submit ourselves to the whole Church, as the witness and keeper of the Scriptures, and judge of the Faith.

I do not often speak to you, at least I try to avoid speaking to you, of such things as these: but there are many tempters abroad, who think they do God service by unsettling our minds, and making us discontented with our Church; and I thought it might be well, for once and away, to try and explain to you one plain rule, by which even an unlearned man' may see that ours is the safest way : seeing that we depend, not each man on himself, nor all on one single Bishop, but each and all upon that Body, with which Christ has promised to be even unto the end of the world. Plainly, then, an unlearned person is safe in communion with our Church, if only he abide in that communion worthily. For he receives the whole Bible according to the Creeds, according to the interpretation which the Church has put on it from the beginning. He keeps that old commandment concerning which S. John has said, that if it remain in us, we abide in the Son and in the Father. This is a great and aweful privilege. O let us see to it, my brethren, that we forfeit it not. What will it avail us to hold the Catholic Faith, to believe rightly of the Trinity and the Incarnation, if in our lives we give no glory but rather dishonour to the Holy Trinity, if by our sins we cut ourselves off from Him Who was made Man to graft us into Himself? But then, how great a blessing, my brethren, to be freed from the necessity of doubting and arguing on our Faith ! to have accepted once for all the testimony of the whole Church as contained in the Prayer Book, and so to be free to give all one's attention to the keeping of Christ's commandments, and thereby abiding in His Love! Surely, notwithstanding the perplexities and distresses of the time, we Churchmen in England are too happy, if we knew but our own good. Surely the lot has fallen unto us in a fair ground, yea, we have a goodly heritage: only may it please Him to keep us from forfeiting it by sin and unthankfulness!

But while we thus adore and bless our good God and Father for the portion which He has assigned to us, and watch jealously lest we lose any of it, let us beware of rashly judging others, calling them heretics, and saying they are out of the Church. They are heretics, whom the Church has declared to be so: not all, who may seem to us to deserve the name. A man can hardly, I suppose, be a heretic, who receives the Creeds, and desires to submit himself to the Church. He may mistake what the Church says; he may be an erring brother: but he can hardly be a heretic.

Be very gentle, then, in your judgement of those who differ: but be very jealous, I say it again, be very jealous for the ancient Truth; do not either depart from it yourself, or willingly let others forsake it, who depend on you. The Creeds, the Catechism, the Sacramental Offices of the Church, are a precious treasure; they are, as it were, ten talents, which God hath entrusted to the care of every one of us: how dreadful to scorn and cause them to be blasphemed by any evil living of ours! How dangerous to hide them in a napkin or to bury them! Tenfold more so than in him who had but one talent!

And one thing more. If we considered as we ought what the word Catholic means, it would make our hearts burn within us with something, a little, a very little like the zeal of a faithful missionary. Our Saviour Who died for us, He Who is our God and our All, He hath in every way declared His will that His kingdom should be universal, that His promise should be both for Jews and Gentiles: and we too, brethren, if we at all have the mind of Christ, how can we help longing for the day, when the kingdoms of this world shall all of them become His kingdoms, when His way shall be known upon earth, His saving health among all nations? And if we long for it, how can we help thinking often, and praying often, for that happy day? And if we think of it and pray for it, how can we be other than glad and thankful, when our Lord gives us a chance to do some little good in that way, by giving of our subtance for missionary work, though it be but a farthing, and we can but ill spare it? O my brethren, it is a great thing, a rare privilege, a precious blessing, to be a fellow-worker with God in saving souls: do not you throw it away. As you remember the kingdom of heaven every time you say your prayers, for you always say, 'Thy kingdom come,' so never allow yourselves to forget it in the ordering of your daily life. Give what you can towards it; set it up more and more in your own heart and in your own house: if you have any depending on you, as children or servants, do your very best to make and keep them true subjects of that kingdom: pray and strive to have a Catholic spirit towards all men, a spirit of universal love; bear with their infirmities; make the most of their good intentions and beginnings: hope the best: despair of no one, for at least you can always go on praying for him. And when you are tempted to give any one up; think with yourself, What would have become of me, if Jesus Christ, the Good Shepherd, had given me up?

Thus will you be true Catholic Christians here, and by the grace of God, happy spirits in heaven.

SERMON XII[a].

THE CHURCH APOSTOLIC.

DEUT. v. 31.

Stand thou here by Me, and I will speak unto thee all the commandments.

THIS verse is a figure of what should be God's way of dealing with us in the Christian Church. He was to be the One Teacher and Governor in it, yet He was to teach and govern by certain whom He would choose. Accordingly we find, that as the first word in the Creed concerning the Church is One; the second, Catholic; so the third word is Apostolic. It is one, because our Saviour is One: Catholic, because He is the Saviour of all men. Why, and in what respects, is it Apostolic? The meaning of the word is, as you know, somewhat belonging to the Apostles. And who are the Apostles? Messengers of Christ: persons sent by Him with a special commission to say and do certain things in His Name. And the things they were appointed to do are the very things by which we are, one by one, united to Christ, and kept in union and

[a] *Marked*, 'Catech. on the Church 3.'

communion with Him. So that if one would be reasonably sure of belonging to Christ, and being in a way to be saved by Him, he must have a reasonable hope that he is in that company and brotherhood which began in the holy Apostles on the Day of Pentecost: that he continues as did those first Christians, in the Apostles' fellowship.

And of this, by God's special mercy, we may be reasonably sure, each one for himself. We are not to doubt, but earnestly to believe it. For, first of all, we know quite for certain who the Apostles were, how and when appointed, and with what message, on what errand, Christ sent them. That there might be no doubt, their names are set down in three out of the four Gospels, and in the Acts of the Apostles. They were ordained by our Lord Himself, under the title of Apostles, after a night spent in prayer, and had a solemn charge given to them. They were in such constant attendance on Him, that there could be no mistaking them, who they were; all that had knowledge of Jesus Himself might take knowledge of them, that they had been with Jesus. They were twelve in number, to answer to the twelve tribes of Israel: whereby we may understand that in them was gathered up, as it were, the whole people of God, His new Israel, to be entrusted with His new law. They were to be a sort of twelve Patriarchs, like the twelve sons of Jacob, through whom the special blessings of God were to be conveyed to His spiritual children through all ages and in all lands. Nothing could be plainer than that they are God's messengers; nothing greater or more solemn than their message. It was, in a word, to be as Christ in the world. So it was delivered to them, the very first time they saw our Lord after His Resurrection. 'ᵇ As My Father hath sent Me, even so send I you.' His Father had sent Him to be Prophet, Priest, and King over His people: and now He sends His Apostles in like manner. They too were in their measure to do the work of prophets, priests, and kings in the Church. They were to be prophets, because the Holy Ghost should come and guide them into all truth. They were to be priests, because He said to them, 'ᶜ Do this in remembrance of Me:' i.e. 'Make the bread and wine Christ's Body and Blood, as I have now done; and offer it to the Father in union with the perpetual Memorial of My Death, which I shall be offering to Him in Heaven.' They were to be kings, lawgivers, and judges in the Church, because He said, 'ᵈ I appoint unto you a kingdom, as My Father hath appointed unto Me;' and, 'ᵉ When the Son of Man shall sit in the throne of His Glory, ye also shall sit upon twelve thrones, judging the twelve tribes of

ᵇ S. John xx. 21.   ᶜ S. Luke xxii. 19.   ᵈ Ib. 29.
ᵉ S. Matt. xix. 28.

Israel;' and, 'f I will give unto thee the keys of the kingdom of heaven, and whatsoever thou shalt bind on earth shall be bound in Heaven, and whatsoever thou shalt loose on earth shalt be loosed in Heaven:' and, 'g Whose soever sins ye remit, they are remitted unto them, and whose soever sins ye retain, they are retained.' And once for all He gave the word to S. Peter, and through him to all the rest, 'h Feed My sheep;' and, 'Feed My Lambs.' Thus you see the whole Church, and all matters relating to it, were entrusted to the Apostles; and that all the rest might obey them, it was said, 'i He that heareth you heareth Me, and he that despiseth you despiseth Me:' or as S. John said long afterwards, 'j We are of God: he that knoweth God heareth us; he that is not of God heareth not us.' The Apostles therefore were kings to rule the Church, as well as priests to offer up its spiritual sacrifices, and prophets to teach its doctrines.

It is true that in a certain sense all Christians are kings and priests, and all the Lord's people are prophets: as S. Peter says, He hath made us 'k a royal priesthood, an holy nation, a peculiar people;' and S. John, He hath 'l loved us, and washed us from our sins in His own Blood, and hath made us kings and

---

f S. Matt. xvi. 19. g S. John xx. 23. h Ib. xxi. 15-17.
i S. Luke x. 16. j 1 S. John iv. 6. k 1 S. Pet. ii. 9.
l Rev. i. 5.

priests unto God and His Father;' and Isaiah, '[m] All thy children shall be taught of the Lord.' Yes, brethren, we are all kings and priests, because we are all members of Him, Who is the true King and Priest: we are kings, to rule over our own wild passions and fancies: we are priests to offer ourselves, our souls and bodies, a living sacrifice to God, and join in offering the Church's perpetual Sacrifice, which is her Lord's Body and Blood: but this hinders not but that there should be among us an especial order of men, whose business it is to govern the Church in His Name, and to offer up to His Father His appointed memorials; to bless us, and to intercede for us. The Jewish people were called by the Lord on Mount Sinai, '[n] a kingdom of priests and a holy nation,' yet they had special kings, as David, and priests, as Aaron, on whose office no one else might intrude. As S. Paul, speaking of the priest's office, says to the Hebrews, '[o] No man taketh this honour unto himself, but he that is called of God, as was Aaron.' And we know what fearful things happened to Korah and his company, who set themselves up as if they might be priests as well as Aaron. The fire came out from the Lord, and consumed them; and as for those who took part with them, the earth opened her mouth and swallowed them up. Yet the word which they spoke was in itself true:

[m] Is. liv. 13.   [n] Ex. xix. 6.   [o] Heb. v. 4.

'ᴾ All the congregation are holy, every one of them, and the Lord is among them.' But they would not receive what God had so plainly taught them, that His Will nevertheless was to have certain special priests among them, Aaron and his family, who only might offer incense. The whole Church, both Jewish and Christian, were to be priests, yet the outward work of priests was always to be done by persons especially ordained for it. Much in the same way as the whole of a man sees and hears things, but he sees them only with his eyes, and hears things, but only with his ears; so the whole Church sacrifices, and blesses, but it is only through her priests; the whole Church confirms and ordains, but it is only through her Bishops.

I say, through her Bishops: for this is the way in which the present Church may be truly called Apostolic; this is how it has fellowship with the Apostles, though the last of them has now been dead more than seventeen hundred and fifty years. The Bishops stand in their place. E. g. before S. Paul died, he laid his hands on Timothy, to make him Bishop of Ephesus; and on Titus, to make him Bishop of Crete: and so in other places, he and other Apostles did the like: and these persons, so made Bishops, stood in the place of the Apostles, and had power to do what they did: to confirm, ordain priests, consecrate other

ᵖ Num. xvi. 3.

Bishops, govern the Churches, be judges in all Church matters. And they, before they died, laid hands upon others to be Bishops when they should be gone: and they upon others; quite down to our time: and so the providence of God has kept up a constant chain or succession of Bishops, i. e. of persons coming in the place of the Apostles, ever since S. Peter's time and S. Paul's: just as the same Providence has kept up the succession of the plants and animals after their kind, from the day in which they were first created; just as it kept up the chain or succession of Jewish priests in the family of Aaron. Only that succession was kept up in the way of natural birth; this, by laying on of hands. No man might be a priest among the Jews, except he could make out his descent from Aaron: no man may be a priest or Bishop among Christians, except he can show that he was ordained by one, who, by laying on of hands, had inherited from the Holy Apostles authority to ordain. Thus each new generation of Bishops may be called in some sense the *spiritual* parents of the next generation: as Aaron was the *natural* parent of all the Jewish priests. Where such Bishops are, maintaining entire Christ's holy Creed, there is Christ's Church, and there is Christ Himself: and well is it for those who, by God's great and distinguishing mercy, are members, perhaps hardly knowing it themselves, of such a body as this.

They must not doubt but earnestly believe, that theirs is a portion of the One Holy Church Universal: and if they do not put themselves out by their sins, assuredly they are 'very members ingrafted into the mystical Body of Christ, which is the blessed company of God's faithful people; and are also heirs through hope of His everlasting kingdom, by the merits of the most precious Death and Passion of His dear Son.'

Now this, my brethren, is the privilege of each one of us. For the Church of England, that portion of the Church, to which we, by God's mercy, belong, is as surely as any in the world tied to the Apostles by the Bishops. We e. g. in this village have our Bishop, the Bishop of Winchester: and we can trace up each link in the chain of his succession quite back to the time of the Apostles, just as certainly as we can trace the natural descent of our Queen Victoria from the old kings and queens of England. We have a Bishop, and in many ways the good providence of God is from time to time showing us how we are tied to him, and through him to the Apostles and to Christ Himself. Most of you may remember his coming here, when this Church was newly built and fitted up, to bless and consecrate it in the name of Jesus Christ. Why? Because it was always held right in the Church, that places as well as persons, Churches as well as Clergymen, should not be set apart to God's special service, without a solemn dedication and blessing from one of those who are as God's high priests among men. The Bishop's blessing on that day was the sign and token of Jesus Christ coming to dwell in His Temple. Again, we remember more than once the Bishop coming here to confirm : we remember, the greater part of us, each one his own Confirmation. Now, what recollection is *that*, would we but in earnest apply our minds to it, and think of it as it really was! We saw indeed but the venerable presence of an earthly father and high priest; we felt but his hand overshadowing us when we were on our knees before him : but faith, my brethren, true Christian faith, if it was then living and working in our hearts, caused us to see with our mind's eye something far greater and more blessed : Jesus Christ invisibly present; (for to our Bishop as well as to all other Bishops His promise was given, 'q I am with you always, even unto the end of the world.') He was present therefore with the Bishop confirming us, as He had been with the Priest or Deacon taking us up in his arms at our Christening. With the eye of faith (if we were not faithless, but believing) we then saw approaching to us, as we knelt, the great Shepherd and Bishop of our souls. His own Divine, Blessed, Loving Right Hand, we felt it laid upon our head: and it was strength and comfort and effectual help to us, and has

q S. Matt. xxviii. 20.

been ever since, in our hard fight against the world, the flesh, and the devil. Thus, I am sure, it has been, in a greater or less degree, with all among us who came to be confirmed, in faith. They were aware of their Saviour drawing very near them: and whether we knew it or no, my brethren, be sure of it, there He was: for it is His promise to His One Catholic and Apostolic Church, to be with His Apostles and their successors when they bless in His Name. And this very year we may expect him. In a few months time, please God, the Bishop will be here, and his and our unseen Master will be with him, to the blessing, strengthening and refreshing, of those who shall kneel before him with devout and dutiful hearts: and to the shame, condemnation, and great loss, of the careless, irreverent, and unbelieving. And surely our hearts, the hearts I mean of those who have been already confirmed, must be very hard and cold, if we are not moved by the thought of Jesus Christ so coming among us, to serious consideration how it was with us when we knelt before Him to be blessed, and how it has been with us ever since.

But we need not wait for such rare occasions as a Church-consecration, or a Confirmation, to be put in mind how great a thing it is for us, that this our Holy Church is Apostolic. For in truth we are (if we would consider) put in mind of it, whenever we come in the way of a clergyman, an ordained minister of Christ. Every clergymen, as such; every Priest or Deacon saying prayers or preaching in Church, or visiting the sick, or administering either of the Sacraments, or privately reproving or comforting or instructing any in Christ's name, he too is a living and moving token of our Lord's Presence. For from some one of the Bishops, the Apostles' successors, he received a call to do these things; and by virtue of our Lord's promise to His Apostles, he goes about doing them, and his doings are indeed a most serious concern, both to himself and others: for the Lord, Who is with him, is both to him and his flock either a savour of death unto death, or else a savour of life unto life. Where Christ takes part, the matter cannot be indifferent nor safely put by, as of small consequence. God give us grace to consider well, both *what* we say and do, and *how* we say it and do it: that His coming among us by His ministers continually may be for joy and not for grief. Depend upon it, the presence of Christ's clergy is one of our chiefest spiritual blessings, not *outwardly* only, not for peace and order only, but inwardly and spiritually; a true token to faithful men of our exceeding nearness to Christ. Surely we have need to go about, as the Israelites ought to have done in the desert: in fear and trembling, in awe and veneration, feeling that the Glory of God is all around us, and might break out at any moment. Christ risen, and especially present among us by His ministers, how can we remember Him, but with fear and great joy? And if we are used to such thoughts, in our dealings with the ministers of Christ, it will help us to be very dutiful in the other parts of our behaviour. And He will graciously fulfil in us, what He promised to His ancient elect people, when they were on their way in the wilderness: '[r] My Presence shall go with thee, and I will give thee rest.'

[r] Ex. xxxiii. 14.

SERMON XIII[a].

THE CHURCH HOLY.

DEUT. vii. 6.

Thou art an holy people unto the Lord thy God.

THE Church in which we believe is *One*, it is *Catholic*, it is *Apostolic*. So far, we have tried to understand what it is: and we have seen partly, what reason we have, as children of the Church of England in particular, to bless the Lord for making us, before we could do anything for ourselves, partakers of these good gifts. Now we come to the fourth word, Holy, which is indeed the greatest and most sacred description of all; for it is the title of God Himself, the Title by which especially He delights to be called. The Angels in heaven, who praise Him day and night, the Cherubim with their many wings and many eyes, who never rest from their work of adoration, say not, over and over, the words Great, or Good, or Almighty, or Glorious, or any of the other names of honour, which may be found ascribed to God in the

[a] *Marked*, 'Catech. on the Church 4.'

Scriptures; but the word which they never tire of repeating is, Holy: '^bHoly, Holy, Holy, Lord God Almighty, which was, and is, and is to come.' '^cHoly, Holy, Holy, is the Lord of Hosts, the whole earth is full of His glory.' And the prophet David, speaking by the Spirit of God, invites us again and again to worship and adore Him on this special ground, that He is Holy. '^dO magnify the Lord our God, and fall down before His footstool, for He is Holy: worship Him upon His holy hill, for the Lord our God is Holy.' The word Holy, then, is that special title, or word of praise, which the word of God applies to the Lord Himself: and when any person or anything else is called holy, it must be because that thing or that person does somehow pertain especially to God. It belongs to God, or it is like unto God: there is something of God in it, which all who fear God or care for Him must acknowledge: and therefore we are to account them holy. Everything is holy, so far forth as it belongs to God, and partakes of Him. This you will plainly see, if you consider how the word 'holy' is used in the Bible, and also how we commonly employ it in our way of talking and writing about things. The Bible, as you have heard this very day, calls all Israel a holy people. 'Thou art an holy people unto the Lord thy God.'

^b Rev. iv. 8.   ^c Is. vi. 3.   ^d Ps. xcix. 5, 9.

So speaks the Almighty by Moses to all Israel, in the last year of their abode in the desert, when they were on the very borders of the land of Canaan. Was it that they had gone on so very well; that they had behaved themselves worthily of God; that He had no great fault to find with them? Far from it, alas! During all those forty years they had been by their sins tempting and proving Him continually, as we are put in mind every morning, in the ninety-fifth Psalm. They, the very persons to whom here it is said, 'Thou art an holy people;' are very soon afterwards called a stiff-necked generation; they had been rebellious against God, from the first day that Moses knew them. How then could they be called holy? It is presently explained: 'The Lord thy God hath chosen thee to be a special people unto Himself, above all people that are upon the face of the earth.' This He did solemnly and publicly, in the sight of men and Angels, in the hearing of heaven and earth, when they were on their way through the wilderness, and He met them in mount Horeb. They were then made and declared holy by an especial covenant, which was sealed between God and them by the sacrifice offered in the Mount. They said, 'All that the Lord commandeth we will do:' and He said, '*Ye shall be unto Me a kingdom of priests and a

* Ex. xix 6.

holy nation.' One might have supposed that they had forfeited this promise by their forty years well nigh spent in murmuring, unbelief, and disobedience. But you see the same gracious word 'holy' is still applied to them. They are still a holy people, notwithstanding their many sins: because God's mark was still upon them; He had not yet left off counting them His own. And so all through the Old Testament, the things that are God's own, set apart for Him, have this title of 'holy' given to them, whether there is any real goodness in them, or no. Thus creatures which have no life or no reason, mere *things*, which could neither obey nor disobey Him, because they could have no doings of their own, are called holy, just because He had vouchsafed to take them for His own. Thus Palestine is called the Holy Land; Jerusalem the Holy city; Zion the Holy mountain; the Tabernacle or temple the Holy place; the furniture of the Altar the holy things; the robes of Aaron and his sons the holy vestments. And we ourselves, as you well know, use the word holy continually in the like meaning. To-day, e. g., and all other Sundays, there is hardly a child here, but if I were to ask him would tell me that they are God's holy days: and if I asked him why, he would go on to say, Because they are God's own days. Again, if you were required to say, what Book is the holiest

The Church Holy.

of all, you would at once say, the Bible, because it is God's own Book; the church, and still more, the chancel, because they are God's own abode, where He presents Himself in a peculiar manner; the Sacraments, because by them He makes us one with Christ and Christ with us: the Clergy, because they are His own servants: and so of everything else: things are holy, according as they belong more entirely to God, or partake more of Him.

For this reason, it could not be, but that the One Catholic Church should be Holy, seeing it is the very Body of Christ on earth, His mystical Body, made up of persons, who are each of them united to Him, members of Him, bone of His Bone, and flesh of His Flesh. As His Natural Soul and Body are beyond compare the holiest things God ever created, for they are taken into union with God Himself: so His Mystical yet real Body, the Church, could not help being Holy, by reason of its nearness to Him. And again, the whole Church, and every member of it, must be holy, by reason of Him, Who came down to dwell in it and in each one, i.e. the Holy Spirit, the Sanctifier, He, by Whom God unites His creatures to Him, and makes them, as far as they may be, partakers of Himself. The Church is Holy, as being the Body of the Most Holy Son, Redeemer of the world: and it is Holy again, as being the abode of the Most Holy Spirit, Sanctifier of the elect. Even as the whole congregation of Israel, and each one of them, was in a very true sense holy, because the Lord was among them, in such sort as He was not among any other people upon earth.

And to this agrees what is said of that Image of God, in which man was at first created. Man was made like God, not only in ruling the creatures, in having reason and understanding, in not being subject to death, but much more, as S. Paul tells us, 'in righteousness and true holiness.' As he was holier, nearer God in other respects than any of God's creatures on earth, so he was, and was to be, holier, nearer to God in goodness and purity, in righteousness and obedience, and in all kinds of heavenly love. This was his true holiness: and when he and we had so miserably forfeited it by wilful sin, He Who by His own Son provided for pardon of our sin, did by His Spirit provide also for our recovering a better holiness even than what we had lost. He gives Himself to us, He comes to us and makes His abode with us, not simply to assure us that we are called and elected, but to endow us with that grace, which will enable us to 'make our calling and election sure.'

The Holy Comforter, the Spirit of God, for Whose coming at Whitsuntide all communicants ought now to be earnestly preparing, He made us holy at first, by uniting us to Jesus Christ in our Baptism, and He longs and desires and is waiting to make us more and more holy, by drawing us continually nearer to Christ, and transforming us into His likeness. But He expects that we in our measure should work with Him and under Him. For so is the Will of God in the whole business of man's salvation. The Lord having done His part, we must do ours. No matter how little, how very insignificant, *that* is which we *can* do: little or much, He has told us to do it, and hath given us strength to fulfil His word. We being once made members of Christ, the Father accounts of us as of persons belonging to Himself; holy, separate from all others. So must we account of ourselves. As He has set us apart from sin and the world, so we must keep ourselves apart. As He offers Himself to us continually in Holy Communion, so must we continually draw near to partake of Him. The Father hath once for all adopted us to be His sons. Can we do less than strive and pray in earnest to be like our Father, a holy family? A holy family! Think, dear brethren, what that expression implies. Would it not have been a strange and fearful thing, beyond all imagination fearful, if our Lord's own near blood-relations, living in the same house with Him, had proved to be wicked, such as Judas? Now why would that have been so very shocking?

Plainly because, being so near to Him, their sin would have been without excuse, the most intolerable affront to Him. Well, if you will believe the Scripture, you must believe that any one of us, wilfully giving way to known sin, is at least as bad, as would have been one of the Holy Family falling away. And on the other hand, if we labour and pray, we are as certain to be helped and favoured as any of those who belonged to the Holy Family.

So the Church prayed and laboured at first: and for many ages it grew wonderfully, and prevailed over the far greater part of the world then known. But now, we have too much cause to fear that there has been and is a great falling off. Men do not now keep themselves so pure, they do not pray and labour as in the primitive Church: therefore (as it seems), the Church does not thrive as at first: there are sad divisions and fallings away, neither do the nations of the world come in quickly, as at the beginning. In S. Paul's time, the unlearned and unbelievers, beholding the order and obedience which was kept up in the Church, were even constrained to fall down and worship God, and report that He was of a truth[f] among the Christians. But now it is much to be feared that our disorder and disobedience is an occasion to many to continue unlearned and unbelievers.

[f] 1 Cor. xiv. 25.

Men say in their hearts, and sometimes with their lips too, How can these be God's own people, whose behaviour has so little of God in it: these, who are, to all outward appearance, so very unlike unto God?

There is but one remedy for this great evil, and *that* is, for Christians to have more faith in their own high and holy calling. Once let us believe that we are holy, in that we are God's own, even more than the children of Israel were, 'a holy nation, a peculiar people,' let us believe this in earnest, and turn our minds continually to it, and we shall surely become holy, in the higher and more perfect sense of the word; we shall be made, by His Almighty Spirit, really and truly like unto God. E. g. suppose a young man believing, heartily and thoughtfully believing, that his own body is holy, even as a church or chancel is holy, because the Holy Ghost has made it His own by coming to dwell in it: such an one will feel that it is just as shocking to sin against his own body, as to deal rudely or profanely with a church or chancel. And believing the same of all other Christians, namely, that their bodies also are temples of the Holy Ghost, he will treat them also with all respect and reverence and purity. Again, if you believe that you and the whole Church are God's peculiar elect people, you must believe that you and all of us, and not the Clergy only, are so far a sort of Priests unto God. And what kind of behaviour do we look for in Priests? Is it not that they should devote themselves, body and soul, to God's service? that they should live and die in the Psalmist's mind, when he said, 'ᵍWhom have I in heaven but Thee: and there is none upon earth that I desire in comparison of Thee?' You are shocked, and think it a grievous scandal, when a minister of God's altar seems to make money or pleasure his god: remember then your own calling, that you too are a priest, called to offer yourself a daily sacrifice to Him: and be afraid and ashamed to go after the world and the flesh. Thus, I think, the simplest of us may plainly feel, that it would greatly help him towards true inward holiness, if he would steadily consider, how holy the Church is, to which by Baptism he belongs, and how frightful a thing it must be for one brought so near God, one who belongs to God in so many ways, one who is a member of Christ, a temple of the Holy Ghost, to lead an unclean, a worldly, a profane life.

The Apostle in his earnest farewell to his Corinthian disciples says, 'ʰExamine yourselves, whether ye be in the faith: prove your own selves. Know ye not your own selves, how that Jesus Christ is in you, except ye be reprobates?' I beseech God to

ᵍ Ps. lxxiii. 24.   ʰ 2 Cor. xiii. 5.

write that word upon all our hearts. As Christians, we have a calling so holy, that, except we be holy ourselves, we are of all men most miserable. As a dead carcase is more loathsome than anything which never was alive, so is a worldly wicked Christian more hateful to God than a heathen. The soul, from which Christ the true life has departed, is more miserable a thousand times than that in which He never abode. Believe this, and strive earnestly to be holy in your lives, as you are holy in your calling. Then, as you are now the sons of God, so, when He shall appear, you shall be like Him. Then are you blessed now, and shall be more and more blessed for ever.

SERMON XIV.

THE COMMUNION OF SAINTS.

S. PHILIP AND S. JAMES' DAY.

S. JAMES i. 18.

Of His own will begat He us with the word of truth, that we should be a kind of first-fruits of His creatures.

OVER and above all the other glorious privileges and tokens, by which our Lord has from the beginning blessed and glorified His Spouse and Body, the Church; that it is One, as being the mystical Body of the One Lord Jesus Christ; Catholic, as belonging alike to all nations; Apostolic, as built upon the foundation of the Apostles and prophets; Holy, as made up of persons entirely dedicated to Him, and meant to be altogether like Him: I say, over and above all these, the Apostles' Creed sets before us two especial privileges and gifts to be found in the Church and nowhere else: the one, the Communion of saints, the other, the Forgiveness of sins. On the one hand, we are brought into nearest communion and intercourse with those who have pleased God from the beginning of the world; the salt of the

The Communion of Saints. 161

earth, the best and holiest of mankind, whether living or in Paradise. On the other hand, there is in the Church, by His exceeding unspeakable mercy, forgiveness and remission of all sins, even the worst: not only forgiveness in Baptism, for whatever has gone before, for all offences committed in men's heathen and unregenerate state: but forgiveness also, entire absolution, for all sins committed after Baptism, but truly and entirely repented of. The holy Church is the mother of us all, but her motherly love is especially shown towards two classes of her children, saints and penitents; the perfect, to help them on towards higher perfection: and the backsliders, to recover them and to welcome them when recovered. Our privilege, my brethren, is exceeding great, whether, having by God's mercy an earnest desire to be perfect, we are encouraged by the assurance that we are in communion with the holy souls of all ages and nations; or whether (as is, alas! far more likely) we have grievously sinned since our Baptism, and can but hope to save our souls so as by fire. The full type and pattern of this our highly favoured calling may be seen in those places, where the holy Gospel sets before us our Lord making Himself a companion of publicans and sinners. 'a Many publicans and sinners drew near, and sat

a S. Matt. ix. 10.

down with Jesus and His disciples.' Then might be seen in one room, at one table, the Holy Saviour of the world, and His saints with Him, and also many who had been living the worst and most discreditable lives: even as in the holy Church and kingdom of the same Saviour, ever since, there has been both the Communion of saints and the Forgiveness of sins: no perfection too high to be hoped for, no sin too bad to be forgiven, if only men would turn to Christ, and dutifully abide with Him.

At present, the plan by which our catechisings have been ordered, would lead us to speak only of the first of these two privileges, the Communion of saints: and this, you will perceive, suits well with the day; for it is a day consecrated to two of the chief of Christ's saints, and the lessons appointed for it, tell us not a little of our Lord's dealings with His saints; what sort of persons they are, whom He commonly chooses out to bring near unto Himself; and in what sort of ways He trains them. He chooses out the simple, teachable, and guileless, and He trains them in temptations, bid them trust Him, and teaches them how to pray. And into communion with such as these He invites us all, even the mere beginners and children, promising continually, You ' [b] shall see greater things than these.'

[b] S. John i. 50.

The Communion of Saints.

It may be well, however, to observe, that the word saints in Scripture does not commonly mean these higher and more perfect Christians: rather it is applied to all Christians whatsoever. The word saints, like the word holy, has two significations, somewhat differing from each other. Sometimes it means all who are holy, in the sense of belonging to God as His peculiar people: sometimes those only who are changed by the Holy Spirit in a remarkable degree, above ordinary Christians. Now in the Acts and in the letters of the Apostles, *all Christians* are called saints. S. Paul directs his letters to the saints in Achaia, the saints of Ephesus, the saints in Colosse[c]: S. Peter, having raised Dorcas from the dead, calls '[d] the *saints* and widows,' and presents her alive. All Christians are called saints, because, whether they be holy or not in their ways, by their calling they are very holy. Thus they are described by S. James, 'Of His own will begat He us with the word of truth, that we should be a kind of first-fruits of His creatures.' First-fruits, i.e. the prime, the very best; as our Lord is entitled, 'The Beginning of the creation of God.' This is the honour, this the mercy, intended by our gracious God for all whom He hath called to be Christians. Not for any desert of theirs, but of His own will, His free love, He would make

[c] 2 Cor. i. 1; Eph. i. 1; Col. i. 2. [d] Acts ix. 41.

them saints, the first-fruits, the best of His creatures; and *that* by giving them a new and heavenly nature, 'begetting them with the Word of His Truth,' i.e. making them partakers, in Baptism, of His Son Jesus Christ, the true and eternal Word. This is S. James' account of all Christians, but it is fulfilled in those only whom the Church acknowledges as saints in an especial sense, because they have gone on unto perfection: saints, such as those who are mentioned in the book of Revelations: worthy to be named along with Apostles and prophets, as being especially like Christ, and especially near to Him. In this meaning we commonly use the word in our times: as when, being so directed by the Church, we put the term Saint before any person's name, as S. Paul, S. John, S. Peter, S. Clement, S. Mary Magdalen: or as when we speak of any dead person, whom we suppose to have been particularly good, as of a departed saint. And so the word is to be taken in the Creed. In very ancient times, the Communion of Saints, in which all Christians believe, was understood to mean communion with those holy ones especially, who have died in the Faith: which we have pledged ourselves to. Not with all Christians, but with good and faithful Christians; nor yet with all good and faithful, but with those of the higher order, who have attained more glorious crowns by their goodness and faithfulness: the best of the good ground, which hath borne fruit a hundred-fold: nor yet equally with all of these, but with those most, whose crown is now sure for ever, because they are no longer on earth, but safe with Him in Paradise. These are they, of whom an ancient Bishop and martyr teaches us to speak and to think on this wise. 'Behold the footmarks left in our sight by the several saints returning into their country, that we, keeping close in their track, might follow them into their joy. Wherefore hasten we not onwards, why do we not quicken our pace, that we may have our true home in sight? There is awaiting us a numerous host of beloved ones; parents, brethren, children very many; a great assembly are longing for us: secure now of their own safety, yet anxious for our salvation. To come to their embrace, to draw near and to be seen of them : how great is the common joy both to them and to us! There is the glorious choir of the Apostles, there the renowned band of rejoicing prophets. There the martyrs, an unnumbered multitude, are wearing the crowns of their victorious conflict. There rejoiceth that brightest assembly of virgins; there is due praise given to the fortitude of those who have confessed Christ[e].' Lift up your hearts, my brethren, think of all these; think

[e] S. Cyprian de mortalit. end, p. 230 Oxf. Tr.

not of them as strangers and afar off: for as it is said of their King and their God, so in a manner it may be said of them—they are not far from every one of us. As surely as we, being Christians, members of the One Body of Christ, have communion with all *Christians* on earth, so surely have we communion also with all the blessed saints departed. Whether they are in paradise or in heaven, they remember and pray for us. An Apostle once, S. John in the sixth chapter of Revelations, saw under the altar, the souls of them that were slain for the Word of God, and for the testimony of His Truth, and heard them praying that God would avenge their blood on them that dwell on the earth [f]. By which we are to understand that the prayers of all saints are being continually offered up for their brethren who are yet here, bearing the burden and heat of the day. They remember us, they pray for us; can it be right for us to forget them? Why even the heathen knew better than that: who in many ways have ever been anxious to do what honour they can to their departed friends. If we turn away from the memory of the dead, we are so far worse than the unbelievers. God keep us from such unnatural, such selfish carelessness! They remember and pray for us: what can we do less than love, long for, and imitate them?

[f] Rev. vi. 9, 10.

As the holy days of the saints come on, one after another, let us endeavour to have a real strong conviction, that they are no strangers, that we are in true fellowship with them. They are in fact nearer to us than any of our friends living here on earth out of our sight. For 'in the midst of life we are in death;' it is close to us, there is but a hair's breadth betwixt us and it: and if we die in God's faith and fear, then, in a moment, in the twinkling of an eye, we are with the saints, with the holy men who were taken to their rest so many years ago, with Abraham, Isaac, and Jacob, whom our Lord honoured by promising that all true believers should sit down with them in His kingdom[g]. Think of the patient beggar Lazarus, in our Saviour's parable: one moment at the gate of the rich man, full of sores[h]: longing for the crumbs, but with no one to look after him (so it seems) but the dogs: the next moment borne on the wings of Angels, more gloriously than all the most glorious on earth, and resting in Abraham's bosom with that rest which remaineth for the people of God. Do not these two conditions seem very far apart one from the other? Yet Lazarus by the grace of God found them to be quite close together. And so, my brethren, it will be with each one of us, if we will but diligently try to walk

[g] S. Matt. viii. 11.   [h] S. Luke xvi. 20-22.

in the steps of the faith of Abraham and Lazarus: we shall find by God's mercy, when our hour of departure comes, that the spirits and souls of the righteous are very near us. We call upon them often in one of our Church hymns, 'O ye spirits and souls of the righteous, bless ye the Lord: praise Him, and magnify Him for ever.' What a thing will it be, my brethren, what a joy and what a wonder, when we shall come not only to believe and hope, but to feel and know that they have been all along joining with us! I say to you then, my brethren, *practise* this faith : try to think of the holy ones departed, as of fellow-travellers got on a little before to the end of a journey which they and you were making in common; a few steps more, and you will be with them, you will see them: they are even now standing on the shore of eternity to welcome you, as the Blessed Jesus on the shore of the lake of Gennesaret[1], when the disciples were drawing near to land after their hard night's toil in fishing. Learn to regard them as really near you; really, and that soon, to be in your sight: and above all things learn to love them; learn truly to love those saints whom you have never yet seen. Indeed, if you will but read and hear and seriously attend, you can hardly choose but love them, so noble and amiable

[1] S. John xxi. 4.

are the things which Holy Scripture tells concerning them. Only be on your guard against this snare, for it is but too common and dangerous; beware of imagining, 'These were saints, great heroes in virtue and piety, pureness and charity, and I am but an ordinary person; well may I admire them, but it is no use pretending to copy them.' Such thoughts are too natural, but they come of the Evil one; put them down altogether, I beseech you: believe that our Saviour was in earnest when He said, '[k]Be ye perfect, as your Father which is in heaven is perfect.' And surely if the Lord's own example is not too high for us to copy, much less is that of His saints. Those great and good and holy ones began as we did, with a fallen and corrupt nature; some of them, like too many of us, were great sinners at some time of their life: they had no other hope of salvation, no other way of salvation than we: as one of the chief of them said, speaking of those who by nature were furthest from God, '[l]we believe that through the grace of the Lord Jesus Christ, we shall be saved, even as they.' Wherefore if we would be saved as the saints are, we must walk in the way of the saints; we must labour to have their mind, and to copy their doings. We must believe that there is such a thing as Christian perfection. Our

[k] S. Matt. v. 48.   [l] Acts xv. 11.

Lord Himself has told us so, instructing us how a man might be perfect, and lay up a rich treasure in heaven [m] : and again telling us of the best of the good ground, which brought forth fruit, not thirty nor sixty but even a hundred-fold [n]; and how one of those who were entrusted with their Master's goods made one pound into ten pounds, another into five only [o]. We must believe this, and we must practise it according to our measure: we must try to do all our duties as well and as perfectly as we can. Else how can we say that we love God with all our strength? How are we not breaking the first and great commandment? A loving mother is not contented to do just a little for her child, she longs to perform all her duties to it as well as ever any mother did. Surely, if we have no such zeal as this towards God, if we are satisfied to be just no worse than the ordinary sort, just good enough, as we think, not to go to hell, we show but too plainly, that our love for Christ is not in reality love; surely we are in danger of the sentence which was pronounced on the unprofitable servant. Our Almighty Friend and Father was not sparing of His mercy to us. He gave us His own, His only Son: He sent down His Spirit to change our hearts; He hath bestowed upon us, freely and richly, all that could work together for our good

[m] S. Matt. xix. 21.   [n] Ib. xiii. 8.   [o] S. Luke xix. 16-18.

both in this world and in the world to come. Alas, that we should be so dead and cold, in the midst of this Divine fire! What if it should prove by and bye, that in our unwillingness to do more than is absolutely necessary, we have fallen away from God's portion altogether—let our lamps go entirely out! For Christ's sake, and for our own soul's sake, let us pray to have better minds.

Precious to the Lord
is the death of His saints.

www.ingramcontent.com/pod-product-compliance
Lightning Source LLC
Chambersburg PA
CBHW032155160426
43197CB00008B/922